AF675239

CONTENTS

1.ARRAY OPERATIONS

1.1. Create, Initialize elements, Insert element, Delete element & Search element in an array

```
#include <iostream>
const int MAX_SIZE = 100; // Maximum size of the array
class ArrayOperations {
private:
    int arr[MAX_SIZE];
    int size;
public:
    // Constructor
    ArrayOperations() : size(0) {}
    // Function to print the array
    void printArray() {
        for (int i = 0; i < size; ++i) {
            std::cout << arr[i] << " ";
        }
        std::cout << std::endl;
    }
    // Function to search for an element in the array
    int searchElement(int element) {
        for (int i = 0; i < size; ++i) {
            if (arr[i] == element) {
                return i; // Return the index if the element is found
            }
        }
        return -1; // Return -1 if the element is not found
    }
    // Function to insert an element at a specified index
    void insertElement(int index, int element) {
        if (size >= MAX_SIZE) {
            std::cout << "Array is full. Cannot insert more elements." << std::endl;
            return;
```

```
    }
    if (index < 0 || index > size) {
        std::cout << "Invalid index for insertion." << std::endl;
        return;
    }
    // Shift elements to make space for the new element
    for (int i = size; i > index; --i) {
        arr[i] = arr[i - 1];
    }
    // Insert the new element
    arr[index] = element;
    // Increment the size of the array
    ++size;
}
// Function to delete an element at a specified index
void deleteElement(int index) {
    if (size <= 0) {
        std::cout << "Array is empty. Cannot delete elements." << std::endl;
        return;
    }
    if (index < 0 || index >= size) {
        std::cout << "Invalid index for deletion." << std::endl;
        return;
    }
    // Shift elements to remove the element at the specified index
    for (int i = index; i < size - 1; ++i) {
        arr[i] = arr[i + 1];
    }
    // Decrement the size of the array
    --size;
}
// Function to initialize elements in the array
void initializeElements() {
```

```
        for (int i = 0; i < 5; ++i) {
            arr[size++] = i * 2;
        }
    }
};
int main() {
    ArrayOperations arrayObj;
    // Initialize elements
    arrayObj.initializeElements();
    // Print the original array
    std::cout << "Original Array: ";
    arrayObj.printArray();
    // Search element
    int searchValue = 6;
    int searchResult = arrayObj.searchElement(searchValue);
    if (searchResult != -1) {
        std::cout << searchValue << " found at index " << searchResult << std::endl;
    } else {
        std::cout << searchValue << " not found in the array." << std::endl;
    }
    // Insert element
    int insertIndex = 2;
    int insertValue = 10;
    arrayObj.insertElement(insertIndex, insertValue);
    std::cout << "After Insertion: ";
    arrayObj.printArray();
    // Delete element
    int deleteIndex = 4;
    arrayObj.deleteElement(deleteIndex);
    std::cout << "After Deletion: ";
    arrayObj.printArray();
    return 0;
}
```

This program defines a ArrayOperations class with member functions for initializing, printing, searching, inserting, and deleting elements in the array. The main function demonstrates how to use these operations on an instance of the class.

1.2. Sum elements in an array

You can create a class in C++ to encapsulate the operations related to an array, including summing its elements. Here's an example:

```
#include <iostream>
const int MAX_SIZE = 100; // Maximum size of the array
class ArrayOperations {
private:
   int arr[MAX_SIZE];
   int size;
public:
   // Constructor
   ArrayOperations() : size(0) {}
   // Function to initialize elements in the array
   void initializeElements() {
      for (int i = 0; i < 5; ++i) {
         arr[size++] = i * 2;
      }
   }
   // Function to print the array
   void printArray() {
      for (int i = 0; i < size; ++i) {
         std::cout << arr[i] << " ";
      }
      std::cout << std::endl;
   }
   // Function to calculate the sum of elements in the array
   int sumElements() {
      int sum = 0;
      for (int i = 0; i < size; ++i) {
         sum += arr[i];
      }
      return sum;
   }
```

```
};
int main() {
    ArrayOperations arrayObj;
    // Initialize elements
    arrayObj.initializeElements();
    // Print the original array
    std::cout << "Original Array: ";
    arrayObj.printArray();
    // Calculate and print the sum of elements
    int sum = arrayObj.sumElements();
    std::cout << "Sum of Elements: " << sum << std::endl;
    return 0;
}
```

In this example, the ArrayOperations class includes a sumElements member function that calculates the sum of elements in the array. The main function demonstrates how to use this function on an instance of the class.

1.3.Average elements in an array

You can create a class in C++ to encapsulate the operations related to an array, including calculating the average of its elements. Here's an example:

```
#include <iostream>
const int MAX_SIZE = 100; // Maximum size of the array
class ArrayOperations {
private:
  int arr[MAX_SIZE];
  int size;
public:
  // Constructor
  ArrayOperations() : size(0) {}
  // Function to initialize elements in the array
  void initializeElements() {
    for (int i = 0; i < 5; ++i) {
      arr[size++] = i * 2;
    }
  }
  // Function to print the array
  void printArray() {
    for (int i = 0; i < size; ++i) {
      std::cout << arr[i] << " ";
    }
    std::cout << std::endl;
  }
  // Function to calculate the average of elements in the array
  double averageElements() {
    if (size == 0) {
      std::cout << "Array is empty. Cannot calculate average." << std::endl;
      return 0.0;
    }
    int sum = 0;
    for (int i = 0; i < size; ++i) {
```

```
            sum += arr[i];
        }
        return static_cast<double>(sum) / size;
    }
};
int main() {
    ArrayOperations arrayObj;
    // Initialize elements
    arrayObj.initializeElements();
    // Print the original array
    std::cout << "Original Array: ";
    arrayObj.printArray();
    // Calculate and print the average of elements
    double average = arrayObj.averageElements();
    std::cout << "Average of Elements: " << average << std::endl;
    return 0;
}
```

In this example, the ArrayOperations class includes an averageElements member function that calculates the average of elements in the array. The main function demonstrates how to use this function on an instance of the class. The function returns a double to allow for fractional averages.

1.4. Find the maximum element in an array

You can create a class in C++ to encapsulate the operations related to an array, including finding the maximum element. Here's an example:

```
#include <iostream>
const int MAX_SIZE = 100; // Maximum size of the array
class ArrayOperations {
private:
   int arr[MAX_SIZE];
   int size;
public:
   // Constructor
   ArrayOperations() : size(0) {}
   // Function to initialize elements in the array
   void initializeElements() {
      for (int i = 0; i < 5; ++i) {
         arr[size++] = i * 2;
      }
   }
   // Function to print the array
   void printArray() {
      for (int i = 0; i < size; ++i) {
         std::cout << arr[i] << " ";
      }
      std::cout << std::endl;
   }
   // Function to find the maximum element in the array
   int findMaxElement() {
      if (size == 0) {
         std::cout << "Array is empty. Cannot find maximum element." << std::endl;
         return INT_MIN; // Return a sentinel value for an empty array
      }
      int maxElement = arr[0];
      for (int i = 1; i < size; ++i) {
```

```
            if (arr[i] > maxElement) {
                maxElement = arr[i];
            }
        }
        return maxElement;
    }
};
int main() {
    ArrayOperations arrayObj;
    // Initialize elements
    arrayObj.initializeElements();
    // Print the original array
    std::cout << "Original Array: ";
    arrayObj.printArray();
    // Find and print the maximum element
    int maxElement = arrayObj.findMaxElement();
    if (maxElement != INT_MIN) {
        std::cout << "Maximum Element: " << maxElement << std::endl;
    }
    return 0;
}
```

In this example, the ArrayOperations class includes a findMaxElement member function that finds the maximum element in the array. The main function demonstrates how to use this function on an instance of the class. The function returns INT_MIN as a sentinel value in case the array is empty.

1.5. Find the minimum element in an array

You can create a class in C++ to encapsulate the operations related to an array, including finding the minimum element. Here's an example:

```
#include <iostream>
#include <climits>
const int MAX_SIZE = 100; // Maximum size of the array
class ArrayOperations {
private:
  int arr[MAX_SIZE];
  int size;
public:
  // Constructor
  ArrayOperations() : size(0) {}
  // Function to initialize elements in the array
  void initializeElements() {
    for (int i = 0; i < 5; ++i) {
      arr[size++] = i * 2;
    }
  }
  // Function to print the array
  void printArray() {
    for (int i = 0; i < size; ++i) {
      std::cout << arr[i] << " ";
    }
    std::cout << std::endl;
  }
  // Function to find the minimum element in the array
  int findMinElement() {
    if (size == 0) {
      std::cout << "Array is empty. Cannot find minimum element." << std::endl;
      return INT_MAX; // Return a sentinel value for an empty array
    }
    int minElement = arr[0];
```

```
        for (int i = 1; i < size; ++i) {
            if (arr[i] < minElement) {
                minElement = arr[i];
            }
        }
        return minElement;
    }
};
int main() {
    ArrayOperations arrayObj;
    // Initialize elements
    arrayObj.initializeElements();
    // Print the original array
    std::cout << "Original Array: ";
    arrayObj.printArray();
    // Find and print the minimum element
    int minElement = arrayObj.findMinElement();
    if (minElement != INT_MAX) {
        std::cout << "Minimum Element: " << minElement << std::endl;
    }
    return 0;
}
```

In this example, the ArrayOperations class includes a findMinElement member function that finds the minimum element in the array. The main function demonstrates how to use this function on an instance of the class. The function returns INT_MAX as a sentinel value in case the array is empty.

1.6. Merge two sorted Arrays

You can create a class in C++ to encapsulate the operations related to merging two sorted arrays. Here's an example:

```
#include <iostream>
const int MAX_SIZE = 100; // Maximum size of the array
class ArrayOperations {
private:
    int arr[MAX_SIZE];
    int size;
public:
    // Constructor
    ArrayOperations() : size(0) {}
    // Function to initialize elements in the array
    void initializeElements(int sortedArr[], int sortedSize) {
        for (int i = 0; i < sortedSize; ++i) {
            arr[size++] = sortedArr[i];
        }
    }
    // Function to print the array
    void printArray() {
        for (int i = 0; i < size; ++i) {
            std::cout << arr[i] << " ";
        }
        std::cout << std::endl;
    }
    // Function to merge another sorted array into the current array
    void mergeSortedArray(int sortedArr[], int sortedSize) {
        int mergedArr[MAX_SIZE];
        int i = 0, j = 0, k = 0;
        // Merge elements in sorted order
        while (i < size && j < sortedSize) {
            if (arr[i] < sortedArr[j]) {
                mergedArr[k++] = arr[i++];
```

```
            } else {
                mergedArr[k++] = sortedArr[j++];
            }
        }
        // Copy the remaining elements from both arrays, if any
        while (i < size) {
            mergedArr[k++] = arr[i++];
        }
        while (j < sortedSize) {
            mergedArr[k++] = sortedArr[j++];
        }
        // Update the current array with the merged array
        size = k;
        for (int m = 0; m < size; ++m) {
            arr[m] = mergedArr[m];
        }
    }
};
int main() {
    ArrayOperations arrayObj1;
    ArrayOperations arrayObj2;
    // Initialize elements in the first array
    int arr1[] = {1, 3, 5, 7, 9};
    int size1 = sizeof(arr1) / sizeof(arr1[0]);
    arrayObj1.initializeElements(arr1, size1);
    // Initialize elements in the second array
    int arr2[] = {2, 4, 6, 8, 10};
    int size2 = sizeof(arr2) / sizeof(arr2[0]);
    arrayObj2.initializeElements(arr2, size2);
    // Print the original arrays
    std::cout << "Array 1: ";
    arrayObj1.printArray();
    std::cout << "Array 2: ";
```

```
    arrayObj2.printArray();
    // Merge the second array into the first array
    arrayObj1.mergeSortedArray(arr2, size2);
    // Print the merged array
    std::cout << "Merged Array: ";
    arrayObj1.printArray();
    return 0;
}
```

In this example, the ArrayOperations class includes a mergeSortedArray member function that merges another sorted array into the current array. The main function demonstrates how to use this function on instances of the class.

2.SEARCHING TECHNIQUES

2.1.Binary search

You can create a class in C++ to encapsulate the binary search operation. Here's an example:

```
#include <iostream>
const int MAX_SIZE = 100; // Maximum size of the array
class BinarySearch {
private:
   int arr[MAX_SIZE];
   int size;
public:
   // Constructor
   BinarySearch() : size(0) {}
   // Function to initialize elements in the array (assumes the array is sorted)
   void initializeElements() {
      for (int i = 0; i < 10; ++i) {
         arr[size++] = i * 2;
      }
   }
   // Function to print the array
   void printArray() {
      for (int i = 0; i < size; ++i) {
         std::cout << arr[i] << " ";
      }
      std::cout << std::endl;
   }
   // Function to perform binary search on the array
   int binarySearch(int target) {
      int low = 0;
      int high = size - 1;
      while (low <= high) {
         int mid = low + (high - low) / 2;
         if (arr[mid] == target) {
```

```
            return mid; // Element found, return its index
        } else if (arr[mid] < target) {
            low = mid + 1; // Search in the right half
        } else {
            high = mid - 1; // Search in the left half
        }
    }
    return -1; // Element not found
  }
};
int main() {
  BinarySearch binarySearchObj;
  // Initialize elements (assuming the array is sorted)
  binarySearchObj.initializeElements();
  // Print the sorted array
  std::cout << "Sorted Array: ";
  binarySearchObj.printArray();
  // Perform binary search
  int target = 6;
  int result = binarySearchObj.binarySearch(target);
  // Print the result
  if (result != -1) {
    std::cout << "Element " << target << " found at index " << result << std::endl;
  } else {
    std::cout << "Element " << target << " not found in the array." << std::endl;
  }
  return 0;}
```

In this example, the BinarySearch class includes a binarySearch member function that performs binary search on a sorted array. The main function demonstrates how to use this function on an instance of the class. The initializeElements function assumes that the array is sorted for the binary search to work correctly.

2.2.Linear search

You can create a class in C++ to encapsulate the linear search operation. Here's an example:

```
#include <iostream>
const int MAX_SIZE = 100; // Maximum size of the array
class LinearSearch {
private:
    int arr[MAX_SIZE];
    int size;
public:
    // Constructor
    LinearSearch() : size(0) {}
    // Function to initialize elements in the array
    void initializeElements() {
        for (int i = 0; i < 10; ++i) {
            arr[size++] = i * 2;
        }
    }
    // Function to print the array
    void printArray() {
        for (int i = 0; i < size; ++i) {
            std::cout << arr[i] << " ";
        }
        std::cout << std::endl;
    }
    // Function to perform linear search on the array
    int linearSearch(int target) {
        for (int i = 0; i < size; ++i) {
            if (arr[i] == target) {
                return i; // Element found, return its index
            }
        }
        return -1; // Element not found
```

```
    }
};
int main() {
    LinearSearch linearSearchObj;
    // Initialize elements
    linearSearchObj.initializeElements();
    // Print the array
    std::cout << "Array: ";
    linearSearchObj.printArray();
    // Perform linear search
    int target = 6;
    int result = linearSearchObj.linearSearch(target);
    // Print the result
    if (result != -1) {
        std::cout << "Element " << target << " found at index " << result << std::endl;
    } else {
        std::cout << "Element " << target << " not found in the array." << std::endl;
    }
    return 0;
}
```

In this example, the LinearSearch class includes a linearSearch member function that performs linear search on an array. The main function demonstrates how to use this function on an instance of the class.

2.3.Quadratic probing

Quadratic probing is a technique used in open addressing for handling collisions in hash tables. Below is an example of how you can implement quadratic probing using a class in C++:

```
#include <iostream>
#include <cmath>
const int TABLE_SIZE = 10;
class HashTable {
private:
   int table[TABLE_SIZE];
   int size;
public:
   HashTable() : size(0) {
      // Initialize the table with -1 to represent an empty slot
      for (int i = 0; i < TABLE_SIZE; ++i) {
         table[i] = -1;
      }
   }
   // Function to print the hash table
   void printTable() {
      for (int i = 0; i < TABLE_SIZE; ++i) {
         if (table[i] != -1) {
            std::cout << "table[" << i << "] = " << table[i] << std::endl;
         }
      }
   }
   // Function to perform quadratic probing and insert an element into the hash table
   void insert(int key) {
      if (size == TABLE_SIZE) {
         std::cout << "Hash table is full. Cannot insert more elements." << std::endl;
         return;
      }
      int index = key % TABLE_SIZE;
```

```
        int originalIndex = index;
        int i = 1;
        while (table[index] != -1) {
            // Quadratic probing: new_index = (original_index + i^2) % TABLE_SIZE
            index = (originalIndex + i * i) % TABLE_SIZE;
            ++i;
        }
        table[index] = key;
        ++size;
    }
    // Function to search for an element using quadratic probing
    int search(int key) {
        int index = key % TABLE_SIZE;
        int originalIndex = index;
        int i = 1;
        while (table[index] != key) {
            // Quadratic probing: new_index = (original_index + i^2) % TABLE_SIZE
            index = (originalIndex + i * i) % TABLE_SIZE;
            // If we reach an empty slot or go through the entire table, the key is not present
            if (table[index] == -1 || i > TABLE_SIZE) {
                return -1;
            }
            ++i;
        }
        return index;
    }
};
int main() {
    HashTable hashTable;
    // Insert elements into the hash table
    hashTable.insert(5);
    hashTable.insert(25);
    hashTable.insert(10);
```

```
    hashTable.insert(20);
    hashTable.insert(15);
    // Print the hash table
    std::cout << "Hash Table:" << std::endl;
    hashTable.printTable();
    // Search for an element using quadratic probing
    int searchKey = 10;
    int searchResult = hashTable.search(searchKey);
    // Print the search result
    if (searchResult != -1) {
        std::cout << "Element " << searchKey << " found at index " << searchResult <<
std::endl;
    } else {
        std::cout << "Element " << searchKey << " not found in the hash table." << std::endl;
    }
    return 0;
}
```

This example includes a HashTable class that uses quadratic probing for collision resolution. The insert function inserts elements into the hash table, and the search function searches for an element using quadratic probing. The printTable function is used to display the contents of the hash table.

2.4. Linear Probing

Linear probing is another technique used in open addressing for handling collisions in hash tables. Below is an example of how you can implement linear probing using a class in C++:

```
#include <iostream>
const int TABLE_SIZE = 10;
class HashTable {
private:
    int table[TABLE_SIZE];
    int size;
public:
    HashTable() : size(0) {
        // Initialize the table with -1 to represent an empty slot
        for (int i = 0; i < TABLE_SIZE; ++i) {
            table[i] = -1;
        }
    }
    // Function to print the hash table
    void printTable() {
        for (int i = 0; i < TABLE_SIZE; ++i) {
            if (table[i] != -1) {
                std::cout << "table[" << i << "] = " << table[i] << std::endl;
            }
        }
    }
    // Function to perform linear probing and insert an element into the hash table
    void insert(int key) {
        if (size == TABLE_SIZE) {
            std::cout << "Hash table is full. Cannot insert more elements." << std::endl;
            return;
        }
        int index = key % TABLE_SIZE;
        // Linear probing: new_index = (original_index + i) % TABLE_SIZE
```

```
        int i = 1;
        while (table[index] != -1) {
            index = (index + i) % TABLE_SIZE;
            ++i;
        }
        table[index] = key;
        ++size;
    }
    // Function to search for an element using linear probing
    int search(int key) {
        int index = key % TABLE_SIZE;
        // Linear probing: new_index = (original_index + i) % TABLE_SIZE
        int i = 1;
        while (table[index] != key) {
            index = (index + i) % TABLE_SIZE;
            // If we reach an empty slot or go through the entire table, the key is not present
            if (table[index] == -1 || i > TABLE_SIZE) {
                return -1;
            }
            ++i;
        }
        return index;
    }
};
int main() {
    HashTable hashTable;
    // Insert elements into the hash table
    hashTable.insert(5);
    hashTable.insert(25);
    hashTable.insert(10);
    hashTable.insert(20);
    hashTable.insert(15);
    // Print the hash table
```

```
    std::cout << "Hash Table:" << std::endl;
    hashTable.printTable();
    // Search for an element using linear probing
    int searchKey = 10;
    int searchResult = hashTable.search(searchKey);
    // Print the search result
    if (searchResult != -1) {
        std::cout << "Element " << searchKey << " found at index " << searchResult <<
std::endl;
    } else {
        std::cout << "Element " << searchKey << " not found in the hash table." << std::endl;
    }
    return 0;
}
```

This example includes a HashTable class that uses linear probing for collision resolution. The insert function inserts elements into the hash table, and the search function searches for an element using linear probing. The printTable function is used to display the contents of the hash table.

3.LINKED LIST

3.1. Create, insert, delete and display operations

Below is an example of a simple linked list implementation in C++ that includes create, insert, delete, and display operations using a class:

```
#include <iostream>
class Node {
public:
    int data;
    Node* next;
    // Constructor
    Node(int value) : data(value), next(nullptr) {}
};
class LinkedList {
private:
    Node* head;
public:
    // Constructor
    LinkedList() : head(nullptr) {}
    // Function to create a new node and add it to the end of the linked list
    void insert(int value) {
        Node* newNode = new Node(value);
        if (head == nullptr) {
            head = newNode;
        } else {
            Node* current = head;
            while (current->next != nullptr) {
                current = current->next;
            }
            current->next = newNode;
        }
    }
    // Function to delete a node with a specific value from the linked list
    void remove(int value) {
```

```
        if (head == nullptr) {
            std::cout << "Linked list is empty. Cannot delete." << std::endl;
            return;
        }
        if (head->data == value) {
            Node* temp = head;
            head = head->next;
            delete temp;
            return;
        }
        Node* current = head;
        while (current->next != nullptr && current->next->data != value) {
            current = current->next;
        }
        if (current->next == nullptr) {
            std::cout << "Value " << value << " not found in the linked list." << std::endl;
            return;
        }
        Node* temp = current->next;
        current->next = current->next->next;
        delete temp;
    }
    // Function to display the linked list
    void display() {
        Node* current = head;
        while (current != nullptr) {
            std::cout << current->data << " ";
            current = current->next;
        }
        std::cout << std::endl;
    }
    // Destructor to free memory occupied by the linked list
    ~LinkedList() {
```

```
        Node* current = head;
        while (current != nullptr) {
            Node* temp = current;
            current = current->next;
            delete temp;
        }
    }
};
int main() {
    LinkedList linkedList;
    // Insert elements into the linked list
    linkedList.insert(10);
    linkedList.insert(20);
    linkedList.insert(30);
    // Display the linked list
    std::cout << "Linked List: ";
    linkedList.display();
    // Insert more elements
    linkedList.insert(40);
    linkedList.insert(50);
    // Display the updated linked list
    std::cout << "Updated Linked List: ";
    linkedList.display();
    // Delete an element
    linkedList.remove(30);
    // Display the updated linked list
    std::cout << "Linked List after deletion: ";
    linkedList.display();
    return 0;
}
```

This program defines a Node class to represent individual nodes in the linked list and a LinkedList class to manage the linked list. The main function demonstrates how to create a linked list, insert elements, delete an element, and display the linked list. The program also includes a destructor in the LinkedList class to free the memory occupied by the linked list when the program exits.

3.2. Perform traversal

Here's an example of a linked list class in C++ that includes traversal operations (both iterative and recursive methods):

```
#include <iostream>
class Node {
public:
    int data;
    Node* next;
    // Constructor
    Node(int value) : data(value), next(nullptr) {}
};
class LinkedList {
private:
    Node* head;
public:
    // Constructor
    LinkedList() : head(nullptr) {}
    // Function to create a new node and add it to the end of the linked list
    void insert(int value) {
        Node* newNode = new Node(value);
        if (head == nullptr) {
            head = newNode;
        } else {
            Node* current = head;
            while (current->next != nullptr) {
                current = current->next;
            }
            current->next = newNode;
        }
    }
    // Function to display the linked list iteratively
    void displayIterative() {
        Node* current = head;
```

```
        while (current != nullptr) {
            std::cout << current->data << " ";
            current = current->next;
        }
        std::cout << std::endl;
    }
    // Function to display the linked list recursively
    void displayRecursive(Node* current) {
        if (current == nullptr) {
            std::cout << std::endl;
            return;
        }
        std::cout << current->data << " ";
        displayRecursive(current->next);
    }
    // Function to perform iterative traversal of the linked list
    void traverseIterative() {
        Node* current = head;
        std::cout << "Iterative Traversal: ";
        while (current != nullptr) {
            std::cout << current->data << " ";
            current = current->next;
        }
        std::cout << std::endl;
    }
    // Function to perform recursive traversal of the linked list
    void traverseRecursive(Node* current) {
        if (current == nullptr) {
            std::cout << std::endl;
            return;
        }
        std::cout << current->data << " ";
        traverseRecursive(current->next);
```

```
    }
    // Function to call iterative traversal
    void traverse() {
        traverseIterative();
        std::cout << "-------------------" << std::endl;
    }
    // Function to call recursive traversal
    void traverseRecursive() {
        std::cout << "Recursive Traversal: ";
        traverseRecursive(head);
        std::cout << "-------------------" << std::endl;
    }
};
int main() {
    LinkedList linkedList;
    // Insert elements into the linked list
    linkedList.insert(10);
    linkedList.insert(20);
    linkedList.insert(30);
    linkedList.insert(40);
    linkedList.insert(50);
    // Display the linked list iteratively
    linkedList.traverse();

    // Display the linked list recursively
    linkedList.traverseRecursive();
    return 0;
}
```

In this example, the LinkedList class includes both iterative (traverseIterative) and recursive (traverseRecursive) traversal methods. The traverse and traverseRecursive functions are used to call these traversal methods, respectively. The program demonstrates how to create a linked list, insert elements, and perform both iterative and recursive traversals.

3.3. Implement a singly linked list

Below is an example of a singly linked list implemented using a class in C++, which includes operations to create, delete, insert, search, and display elements:

```
#include <iostream>
class Node {
public:
    int data;
    Node* next;
    // Constructor
    Node(int value) : data(value), next(nullptr) {}
};
class SinglyLinkedList {
private:
    Node* head;
public:
    // Constructor
    SinglyLinkedList() : head(nullptr) {}
    // Function to insert a new node at the beginning of the linked list
    void insertAtBeginning(int value) {
        Node* newNode = new Node(value);
        newNode->next = head;
        head = newNode;
    }
    // Function to insert a new node at the end of the linked list
    void insertAtEnd(int value) {
        Node* newNode = new Node(value);
        if (head == nullptr) {
            head = newNode;
        } else {
            Node* current = head;
            while (current->next != nullptr) {
                current = current->next;
            }
```

```
        current->next = newNode;
    }
}
// Function to search for a specific value in the linked list
bool search(int value) {
    Node* current = head;
    while (current != nullptr) {
        if (current->data == value) {
            return true; // Element found
        }
        current = current->next;
    }
    return false; // Element not found
}
// Function to delete a node with a specific value from the linked list
void deleteNode(int value) {
    if (head == nullptr) {
        std::cout << "Linked list is empty. Cannot delete." << std::endl;
        return;
    }
    if (head->data == value) {
        Node* temp = head;
        head = head->next;
        delete temp;
        return;
    }
    Node* current = head;
    while (current->next != nullptr && current->next->data != value) {
        current = current->next;
    }
    if (current->next == nullptr) {
        std::cout << "Value " << value << " not found in the linked list." << std::endl;
        return;
```

```
        }
        Node* temp = current->next;
        current->next = current->next->next;
        delete temp;
    }
    // Function to display the linked list
    void display() {
        Node* current = head;
        while (current != nullptr) {
            std::cout << current->data << " ";
            current = current->next;
        }
        std::cout << std::endl;
    }
    // Destructor to free memory occupied by the linked list
    ~SinglyLinkedList() {
        Node* current = head;
        while (current != nullptr) {
            Node* temp = current;
            current = current->next;
            delete temp;
        }
    }
};

int main() {
    SinglyLinkedList linkedList;
    // Insert elements into the linked list
    linkedList.insertAtEnd(10);
    linkedList.insertAtEnd(20);
    linkedList.insertAtEnd(30);
    // Display the linked list
    std::cout << "Linked List: ";
```

```
linkedList.display();
// Insert more elements at the beginning
linkedList.insertAtBeginning(5);
linkedList.insertAtBeginning(15);
// Display the updated linked list
std::cout << "Updated Linked List: ";
linkedList.display();
// Search for an element
int searchValue = 20;
if (linkedList.search(searchValue)) {
    std::cout << "Value " << searchValue << " found in the linked list." << std::endl;
} else {
    std::cout << "Value " << searchValue << " not found in the linked list." << std::endl;
}
// Delete an element
int deleteValue = 15;
linkedList.deleteNode(deleteValue);
// Display the linked list after deletion
std::cout << "Linked List after deletion: ";
linkedList.display();
return 0;}
```

This program defines a Node class to represent individual nodes in the singly linked list and a SinglyLinkedList class to manage the linked list operations. The main function demonstrates how to create a singly linked list, insert elements at the beginning and end, search for an element, delete an element, and display the linked list. The ~SinglyLinkedList destructor is included to free the memory occupied by the linked list when the program exits.

3.4. Implement a doubly linked list

Below is an example of a doubly linked list implemented using a class in C++, which includes operations to create, insert, delete, search, and display elements:

```
#include <iostream>
class Node {
public:
    int data;
    Node* next;
    Node* prev;
    // Constructor
    Node(int value) : data(value), next(nullptr), prev(nullptr) {}
};
class DoublyLinkedList {
private:
    Node* head;
    Node* tail;
public:
    // Constructor
    DoublyLinkedList() : head(nullptr), tail(nullptr) {}
    // Function to insert a new node at the beginning of the doubly linked list
    void insertAtBeginning(int value) {
        Node* newNode = new Node(value);
        if (head == nullptr) {
            head = tail = newNode;
        } else {
            newNode->next = head;
            head->prev = newNode;
            head = newNode;
        }
    }
    // Function to insert a new node at the end of the doubly linked list
    void insertAtEnd(int value) {
        Node* newNode = new Node(value);
```

```
    if (head == nullptr) {
        head = tail = newNode;
    } else {
        newNode->prev = tail;
        tail->next = newNode;
        tail = newNode;
    }
}
// Function to search for a specific value in the doubly linked list
bool search(int value) {
    Node* current = head;
    while (current != nullptr) {
        if (current->data == value) {
            return true; // Element found
        }
        current = current->next;
    }
    return false; // Element not found
}
// Function to delete a node with a specific value from the doubly linked list
void deleteNode(int value) {
    if (head == nullptr) {
        std::cout << "Doubly linked list is empty. Cannot delete." << std::endl;
        return;
    }
    Node* current = head;
    while (current != nullptr && current->data != value) {
        current = current->next;
    }
    if (current == nullptr) {
        std::cout << "Value " << value << " not found in the doubly linked list." << std::endl;
        return;
    }
```

```
        if (current->prev != nullptr) {
            current->prev->next = current->next;
        } else {
            head = current->next;
        }
        if (current->next != nullptr) {
            current->next->prev = current->prev;
        } else {
            tail = current->prev;
        }
        delete current;
    }
    // Function to display the doubly linked list from head to tail
    void displayForward() {
        Node* current = head;
        while (current != nullptr) {
            std::cout << current->data << " ";
            current = current->next;
        }
        std::cout << std::endl;
    }
    // Function to display the doubly linked list from tail to head
    void displayBackward() {
        Node* current = tail;
        while (current != nullptr) {
            std::cout << current->data << " ";
            current = current->prev;
        }
        std::cout << std::endl;
    }
    // Destructor to free memory occupied by the doubly linked list
    ~DoublyLinkedList() {
        Node* current = head;
```

```
        while (current != nullptr) {
            Node* temp = current;
            current = current->next;
            delete temp;
        }
    }
};
int main() {
    DoublyLinkedList doublyLinkedList;
    // Insert elements into the doubly linked list
    doublyLinkedList.insertAtEnd(10);
    doublyLinkedList.insertAtEnd(20);
    doublyLinkedList.insertAtEnd(30);
    // Display the doubly linked list forward
    std::cout << "Doubly Linked List (Forward): ";
    doublyLinkedList.displayForward();
    // Display the doubly linked list backward
    std::cout << "Doubly Linked List (Backward): ";
    doublyLinkedList.displayBackward();
    // Insert more elements at the beginning
    doublyLinkedList.insertAtBeginning(5);
    doublyLinkedList.insertAtBeginning(15);
    // Display the updated doubly linked list forward
    std::cout << "Updated Doubly Linked List (Forward): ";
    doublyLinkedList.displayForward();
    // Display the updated doubly linked list backward
    std::cout << "Updated Doubly Linked List (Backward): ";
    doublyLinkedList.displayBackward();
    // Search for an element
    int searchValue = 20;
    if (doublyLinkedList.search(searchValue)) {
        std::cout << "Value " << searchValue << " found in the doubly linked list." << std::endl;
    } else {
```

```
        std::cout << "Value " << searchValue << " not found in the doubly linked list." <<
std::endl;
    }
    // Delete an element
    int deleteValue = 15;
    doublyLinkedList.deleteNode(deleteValue);
    // Display the doubly linked list forward after deletion
    std::cout << "Doubly Linked List (Forward) after deletion: ";
    doublyLinkedList.displayForward();
    // Display the doubly linked list backward after deletion
    std::cout << "Doubly Linked List (Backward) after deletion: ";
    doublyLinkedList.displayBackward();
    return 0;
}
```

This program defines a Node class to represent individual nodes in the doubly linked list and a DoublyLinkedList class to manage the doubly linked list operations. The main function demonstrates how to create a doubly linked list, insert elements at the beginning and end, search for an element, delete an element, and display the doubly linked list both forward and backward. The ~DoublyLinkedList destructor is included to free the memory occupied by the doubly linked list when the program exits.

3.5.Reverse a linked list

Reversing a linked list involves changing the direction of links between nodes. Here's an example of how you can reverse a singly linked list using a class in C++:

```
#include <iostream>
class Node {
public:
    int data;
    Node* next;
    // Constructor
    Node(int value) : data(value), next(nullptr) {}
};
class SinglyLinkedList {
private:
    Node* head;
public:
    // Constructor
    SinglyLinkedList() : head(nullptr) {}
    // Function to insert a new node at the beginning of the linked list
    void insertAtBeginning(int value) {
        Node* newNode = new Node(value);
        newNode->next = head;
        head = newNode;
    }
    // Function to display the linked list
    void display() {
        Node* current = head;
        while (current != nullptr) {
            std::cout << current->data << " ";
            current = current->next;
        }
        std::cout << std::endl;
    }
    // Function to reverse the linked list
```

```
    void reverse() {
        Node* prev = nullptr;
        Node* current = head;
        Node* next = nullptr;
        while (current != nullptr) {
            next = current->next;
            current->next = prev;
            prev = current;
            current = next;
        }
        head = prev;
    }
    // Destructor to free memory occupied by the linked list
    ~SinglyLinkedList() {
        Node* current = head;
        while (current != nullptr) {
            Node* temp = current;
            current = current->next;
            delete temp;
        }
    }
};
int main() {
    SinglyLinkedList linkedList;
    // Insert elements into the linked list
    linkedList.insertAtBeginning(10);
    linkedList.insertAtBeginning(20);
    linkedList.insertAtBeginning(30);
    linkedList.insertAtBeginning(40);
    linkedList.insertAtBeginning(50);
    // Display the original linked list
    std::cout << "Original Linked List: ";
    linkedList.display();
```

```
    // Reverse the linked list
    linkedList.reverse();
    // Display the reversed linked list
    std::cout << "Reversed Linked List: ";
    linkedList.display();
    return 0;
}
```

In this example, the SinglyLinkedList class includes a reverse function that reverses the linked list in-place. The main function demonstrates how to create a singly linked list, insert elements at the beginning, display the original linked list, reverse it, and display the reversed linked list. The ~SinglyLinkedList destructor is included to free the memory occupied by the linked list when the program exits.

3.6.Detecting loop in a linked list

Detecting a loop in a linked list can be done using Floyd's Cycle Detection Algorithm, also known as the "tortoise and hare" algorithm. Here's an example of how you can implement loop detection in a singly linked list using a class in C++:

```
#include <iostream>
class Node {
public:
    int data;
    Node* next;
    // Constructor
    Node(int value) : data(value), next(nullptr) {}
};
class SinglyLinkedList {
private:
    Node* head;
public:
    // Constructor
    SinglyLinkedList() : head(nullptr) {}
    // Function to insert a new node at the beginning of the linked list
    void insertAtBeginning(int value) {
        Node* newNode = new Node(value);
        newNode->next = head;
        head = newNode;
    }
    // Function to create a loop in the linked list (for testing purposes)
    void createLoop() {
        if (head == nullptr) {
            std::cout << "Linked list is empty. Cannot create a loop." << std::endl;
            return;
        }
        Node* tail = head;
        while (tail->next != nullptr) {
            tail = tail->next;
```

```
        }
        // Creating a loop by connecting the last node to the second node
        tail->next = head->next;
    }
    // Function to detect a loop in the linked list
    bool detectLoop() {
        Node* slow = head;
        Node* fast = head;
        while (fast != nullptr && fast->next != nullptr) {
            slow = slow->next;
            fast = fast->next->next;
            if (slow == fast) {
                return true; // Loop detected
            }
        }
        return false; // No loop detected
    }
    // Function to display the linked list
    void display() {
        Node* current = head;
        int count = 0;
        while (current != nullptr && count < 10) {
            std::cout << current->data << " ";
            current = current->next;
            count++;
        }
        std::cout << std::endl;
    }
    // Destructor to free memory occupied by the linked list
    ~SinglyLinkedList() {
        Node* current = head;
        while (current != nullptr) {
            Node* temp = current;
```

```
            current = current->next;
            delete temp;
        }
    }
};
int main() {
    SinglyLinkedList linkedList;
    // Insert elements into the linked list
    linkedList.insertAtBeginning(10);
    linkedList.insertAtBeginning(20);
    linkedList.insertAtBeginning(30);
    linkedList.insertAtBeginning(40);
    linkedList.insertAtBeginning(50);
    // Display the linked list
    std::cout << "Linked List: ";
    linkedList.display();
    // Create a loop in the linked list (for testing purposes)
    linkedList.createLoop();
    // Detect a loop in the linked list
    if (linkedList.detectLoop()) {
        std::cout << "Loop detected in the linked list." << std::endl;
    } else {
        std::cout << "No loop detected in the linked list." << std::endl;
    }

    return 0;
}
```

In this example, the SinglyLinkedList class includes a detectLoop function that implements Floyd's Cycle Detection Algorithm. The createLoop function is used to create a loop in the linked list for testing purposes. The main function demonstrates how to create a singly linked list, insert elements at the beginning, display the linked list, create a loop, and detect the loop in the linked list. The ~SinglyLinkedList destructor is included to free the memory occupied by the linked list when the program exits.

3.7. Removing loops in a linked list

Removing loops in a linked list can be done by detecting and breaking the loop. Here's an example of how you can remove loops in a singly linked list using a class in C++:

```
#include <iostream>
#include <unordered_set>
class Node {
public:
   int data;
   Node* next;
   // Constructor
   Node(int value) : data(value), next(nullptr) {}
};
class SinglyLinkedList {
private:
   Node* head;
public:
   // Constructor
   SinglyLinkedList() : head(nullptr) {}
   // Function to insert a new node at the beginning of the linked list
   void insertAtBeginning(int value) {
      Node* newNode = new Node(value);
      newNode->next = head;
      head = newNode;
   }
   // Function to create a loop in the linked list (for testing purposes)
   void createLoop() {
      if (head == nullptr) {
         std::cout << "Linked list is empty. Cannot create a loop." << std::endl;
         return;
      }
      Node* tail = head;
      while (tail->next != nullptr) {
         tail = tail->next;
```

```
        }
        // Creating a loop by connecting the last node to the second node
        tail->next = head->next;
    }
    // Function to detect a loop in the linked list
    bool detectLoop() {
        Node* slow = head;
        Node* fast = head;
        while (fast != nullptr && fast->next != nullptr) {
            slow = slow->next;
            fast = fast->next->next;
            if (slow == fast) {
                return true; // Loop detected
            }
        }
        return false; // No loop detected
    }
    // Function to remove the loop in the linked list
    void removeLoop() {
        Node* slow = head;
        Node* fast = head;
        Node* prev = nullptr;
        while (fast != nullptr && fast->next != nullptr) {
            prev = slow;
            slow = slow->next;
            fast = fast->next->next;
            if (slow == fast) {
                // Loop detected
                break;
            }
        }
    // If a loop is detected, move one pointer to the head and move both pointers at the same
pace
```

```
        if (slow == fast) {
            slow = head;
            while (slow->next != fast->next) {
                slow = slow->next;
                fast = fast->next;
            }
            // Break the loop
            fast->next = nullptr;
        }
    }
    // Function to display the linked list
    void display() {
        Node* current = head;
        int count = 0;
        while (current != nullptr && count < 10) {
            std::cout << current->data << " ";
            current = current->next;
            count++;
        }
        std::cout << std::endl;
    }
    // Destructor to free memory occupied by the linked list
    ~SinglyLinkedList() {
        Node* current = head;
        while (current != nullptr) {
            Node* temp = current;
            current = current->next;
            delete temp;
        }
    }
};
int main() {
    SinglyLinkedList linkedList;
```

```
    // Insert elements into the linked list
    linkedList.insertAtBeginning(10);
    linkedList.insertAtBeginning(20);
    linkedList.insertAtBeginning(30);
    linkedList.insertAtBeginning(40);
    linkedList.insertAtBeginning(50);
    // Display the linked list
    std::cout << "Linked List: ";
    linkedList.display();
    // Create a loop in the linked list (for testing purposes)
    linkedList.createLoop();
    // Detect a loop in the linked list
    if (linkedList.detectLoop()) {
        std::cout << "Loop detected in the linked list." << std::endl;
        // Remove the loop
        linkedList.removeLoop();
        std::cout << "Loop removed from the linked list." << std::endl;
    } else {
        std::cout << "No loop detected in the linked list." << std::endl;
    }
    return 0;
}
```

In this example, the SinglyLinkedList class includes a removeLoop function that uses Floyd's Cycle Detection Algorithm to detect and remove the loop in the linked list. The createLoop function is used to create a loop in the linked list for testing purposes. The main function demonstrates how to create a singly linked list, insert elements at the beginning, display the linked list, create a loop, detect the loop, and remove the loop in the linked list. The ~SinglyLinkedList destructor is included to free the memory occupied by the linked list when the program exits.

4. SORTING

4.1. Bubble sort

Below is an example of implementing the bubble sort algorithm using a class in C++:

```
#include <iostream>
class BubbleSort {
private:
    int* array;
    int size;
public:
    // Constructor
    BubbleSort(int arr[], int n) {
        size = n;
        array = new int[size];
        for (int i = 0; i < size; ++i) {
            array[i] = arr[i];
        }
    }
    // Function to perform bubble sort
    void sort() {
        for (int i = 0; i < size - 1; ++i) {
            for (int j = 0; j < size - i - 1; ++j) {
                if (array[j] > array[j + 1]) {
                    // Swap array[j] and array[j + 1]
                    int temp = array[j];
                    array[j] = array[j + 1];
                    array[j + 1] = temp;
                }
            }
        }
    }
    // Function to display the sorted array
    void displaySortedArray() {
        std::cout << "Sorted Array: ";
```

```
        for (int i = 0; i < size; ++i) {
            std::cout << array[i] << " ";
        }
        std::cout << std::endl;
    }
    // Destructor
    ~BubbleSort() {
        delete[] array;
    }
};
int main() {
    int arr[] = {64, 34, 25, 12, 22, 11, 90};
    int n = sizeof(arr) / sizeof(arr[0]);
    // Create an instance of the BubbleSort class
    BubbleSort bubbleSortObj(arr, n);
    // Perform bubble sort
    bubbleSortObj.sort();
    // Display the sorted array
    bubbleSortObj.displaySortedArray();
    return 0;
}
```

In this example, the BubbleSort class encapsulates the array and provides member functions for sorting and displaying the sorted array. The sort function implements the bubble sort algorithm, and the displaySortedArray function is responsible for displaying the sorted array.

The main function creates an instance of the BubbleSort class, initializes it with an array, performs bubble sort using the sort function, and then displays the sorted array using the displaySortedArray function. The memory allocated for the array is freed in the class destructor (~BubbleSort).

4.2.Selection sort

Below is an example of implementing the selection sort algorithm using a class in C++:

```
#include <iostream>
class SelectionSort {
private:
    int* array;
    int size;
public:
    // Constructor
    SelectionSort(int arr[], int n) {
        size = n;
        array = new int[size];
        for (int i = 0; i < size; ++i) {
            array[i] = arr[i];
        }
    }
    // Function to perform selection sort
    void sort() {
        for (int i = 0; i < size - 1; ++i) {
            // Find the minimum element in the unsorted part of the array
            int minIndex = i;
            for (int j = i + 1; j < size; ++j) {
                if (array[j] < array[minIndex]) {
                    minIndex = j;
                }
            }
            // Swap the found minimum element with the first element
            int temp = array[i];
            array[i] = array[minIndex];
            array[minIndex] = temp;
        }
    }
```

```
    // Function to display the sorted array
    void displaySortedArray() {
        std::cout << "Sorted Array: ";
        for (int i = 0; i < size; ++i) {
            std::cout << array[i] << " ";
        }
        std::cout << std::endl;
    }
    // Destructor
    ~SelectionSort() {
        delete[] array;
    }
};
int main() {
    int arr[] = {64, 34, 25, 12, 22, 11, 90};
    int n = sizeof(arr) / sizeof(arr[0]);
    // Create an instance of the SelectionSort class
    SelectionSort selectionSortObj(arr, n);
    // Perform selection sort
    selectionSortObj.sort();
    // Display the sorted array
    selectionSortObj.displaySortedArray();
    return 0;
}
```

In this example, the SelectionSort class encapsulates the array and provides member functions for sorting and displaying the sorted array. The sort function implements the selection sort algorithm, and the displaySortedArray function is responsible for displaying the sorted array.

The main function creates an instance of the SelectionSort class, initializes it with an array, performs selection sort using the sort function, and then displays the sorted array using the displaySortedArray function. The memory allocated for the array is freed in the class destructor (~SelectionSort).

4.3.Insertion sort

Below is an example of implementing the insertion sort algorithm using a class in C++:

```
#include <iostream>
class InsertionSort {
private:
   int* array;
   int size;
public:
   // Constructor
   InsertionSort(int arr[], int n) {
      size = n;
      array = new int[size];
      for (int i = 0; i < size; ++i) {
         array[i] = arr[i];
      }
   }
   // Function to perform insertion sort
   void sort() {
      for (int i = 1; i < size; ++i) {
         int key = array[i];
         int j = i - 1;
 // Move elements of array[0..i-1] that are greater than key to one position ahead of their
 current position
         while (j >= 0 && array[j] > key) {
            array[j + 1] = array[j];
            j = j - 1;
         }
         array[j + 1] = key;
      }
   }
   // Function to display the sorted array
   void displaySortedArray() {
```

```
        std::cout << "Sorted Array: ";
        for (int i = 0; i < size; ++i) {
            std::cout << array[i] << " ";
        }
        std::cout << std::endl;
    }
    // Destructor
    ~InsertionSort() {
        delete[] array;
    }
};
int main() {
    int arr[] = {64, 34, 25, 12, 22, 11, 90};
    int n = sizeof(arr) / sizeof(arr[0]);
    // Create an instance of the InsertionSort class
    InsertionSort insertionSortObj(arr, n);
    // Perform insertion sort
    insertionSortObj.sort();
    // Display the sorted array
    insertionSortObj.displaySortedArray();
    return 0;
}
```

In this example, the InsertionSort class encapsulates the array and provides member functions for sorting and displaying the sorted array. The sort function implements the insertion sort algorithm, and the displaySortedArray function is responsible for displaying the sorted array.

The main function creates an instance of the InsertionSort class, initializes it with an array, performs insertion sort using the sort function, and then displays the sorted array using the displaySortedArray function. The memory allocated for the array is freed in the class destructor (~InsertionSort).

4.4. Merge sort

Below is an example of implementing the merge sort algorithm using a class in C++:

```
#include <iostream>
#include <vector>
class MergeSort {
private:
    std::vector<int> array;
public:
    // Constructor
    MergeSort(std::vector<int> arr) : array(arr) {}
    // Function to perform merge sort
    void sort() {
        if (array.size() <= 1) {
            return;
        }
        // Split the array into two halves
        std::size_t middle = array.size() / 2;
        std::vector<int> left(array.begin(), array.begin() + middle);
        std::vector<int> right(array.begin() + middle, array.end());
        // Recursively sort the two halves
        MergeSort leftSorter(left);
        MergeSort rightSorter(right);
        leftSorter.sort();
        rightSorter.sort();
        // Merge the sorted halves
        merge(left, right);
    }
    // Function to merge two sorted arrays
    void merge(const std::vector<int>& left, const std::vector<int>& right) {
        std::size_t leftSize = left.size();
        std::size_t rightSize = right.size();
        std::size_t i = 0, j = 0, k = 0;
        // Merge elements from left and right into the original array
```

```
        while (i < leftSize && j < rightSize) {
            if (left[i] <= right[j]) {
                array[k++] = left[i++];
            } else {
                array[k++] = right[j++];
            }
        }
        // Copy the remaining elements of left (if any)
        while (i < leftSize) {
            array[k++] = left[i++];
        }
        // Copy the remaining elements of right (if any)
        while (j < rightSize) {
            array[k++] = right[j++];
        }
    }
    // Function to display the sorted array
    void displaySortedArray() const {
        std::cout << "Sorted Array: ";
        for (int num : array) {
            std::cout << num << " ";
        }
        std::cout << std::endl;
    }
};
int main() {
    std::vector<int> arr = {64, 34, 25, 12, 22, 11, 90};

    // Create an instance of the MergeSort class
    MergeSort mergeSortObj(arr);
    // Perform merge sort
    mergeSortObj.sort();
    // Display the sorted array
```

```
    mergeSortObj.displaySortedArray();
    return 0;
}
```

In this example, the MergeSort class encapsulates the array and provides member functions for sorting and displaying the sorted array. The sort function implements the merge sort algorithm, and the merge function is responsible for merging two sorted arrays.

The main function creates an instance of the MergeSort class, initializes it with a vector, performs merge sort using the sort function, and then displays the sorted array using the displaySortedArray function.

4.5.Quick sort

Below is an example of implementing the quicksort algorithm using a class in C++:

```
#include <iostream>
#include <vector>
class QuickSort {
private:
    std::vector<int> array;
public:
    // Constructor
    QuickSort(std::vector<int> arr) : array(arr) {}
    // Function to perform quicksort
    void sort() {
        quicksort(0, array.size() - 1);
    }
    // Function to perform quicksort on a specific range of the array
    void quicksort(int low, int high) {
        if (low < high) {
            // Partition the array and get the pivot index
            int pivotIndex = partition(low, high);
            // Recursively sort the two sub-arrays
            quicksort(low, pivotIndex - 1);
            quicksort(pivotIndex + 1, high);
        }
    }
    // Function to partition the array and return the pivot index
    int partition(int low, int high) {
        int pivot = array[high];
        int i = low - 1;
        for (int j = low; j < high; ++j) {
            if (array[j] <= pivot) {
                // Swap array[i+1] and array[j]
                std::swap(array[++i], array[j]);
            }
```

```
        }
        // Swap array[i+1] and array[high] (put the pivot in its correct position)
        std::swap(array[i + 1], array[high]);
        return i + 1;
    }
    // Function to display the sorted array
    void displaySortedArray() const {
        std::cout << "Sorted Array: ";
        for (int num : array) {
            std::cout << num << " ";
        }
        std::cout << std::endl;
    }
};
int main() {
    std::vector<int> arr = {64, 34, 25, 12, 22, 11, 90};
    // Create an instance of the QuickSort class
    QuickSort quickSortObj(arr);
    // Perform quicksort
    quickSortObj.sort();
    // Display the sorted array
    quickSortObj.displaySortedArray();
    return 0;
}
```

In this example, the QuickSort class encapsulates the array and provides member functions for sorting and displaying the sorted array. The sort function implements the quicksort algorithm, and the partition function is responsible for partitioning the array.

The main function creates an instance of the QuickSort class, initializes it with a vector, performs quicksort using the sort function, and then displays the sorted array using the displaySortedArray function.

4.6.Topological sort

Topological sorting is mainly used for scheduling tasks or ordering tasks based on dependencies. Below is an example of implementing topological sort using a class in C++:

```
#include <iostream>
#include <vector>
#include <stack>
#include <unordered_map>
#include <unordered_set>
class Graph {
private:
   std::unordered_map<int, std::vector<int>> adjacencyList;
public:
   // Function to add a directed edge to the graph
   void addEdge(int from, int to) {
      adjacencyList[from].push_back(to);
   }
   // Function to perform topological sort
   void topologicalSortUtil(int vertex, std::unordered_set<int>& visited, std::stack<int>&
result) {
      visited.insert(vertex);
      for (int neighbor : adjacencyList[vertex]) {
         if (visited.find(neighbor) == visited.end()) {
            topologicalSortUtil(neighbor, visited, result);
         }
      }
      result.push(vertex);
   }
   // Function to perform topological sort on the entire graph
   std::vector<int> topologicalSort() {
      std::unordered_set<int> visited;
      std::stack<int> result;
      for (const auto& pair : adjacencyList) {
         int vertex = pair.first;
```

```
        if (visited.find(vertex) == visited.end()) {
            topologicalSortUtil(vertex, visited, result);
        }
    }
    std::vector<int> sortedOrder;
    while (!result.empty()) {
        sortedOrder.push_back(result.top());
        result.pop();
    }
    return sortedOrder;
  }
};
int main() {
  Graph graph;
  // Add directed edges to the graph
  graph.addEdge(5, 2);
  graph.addEdge(5, 0);
  graph.addEdge(4, 0);
  graph.addEdge(4, 1);
  graph.addEdge(2, 3);
  graph.addEdge(3, 1);
  // Perform topological sort
  std::vector<int> sortedOrder = graph.topologicalSort();
  // Display the sorted order
  std::cout << "Topological Sort Order: ";
  for (int vertex : sortedOrder) {
    std::cout << vertex << " ";
  }
  std::cout << std::endl;
  return 0;
}
```

In this example, the Graph class represents a directed graph. The addEdge function is used to add directed edges to the graph. The topologicalSort function performs a topological sort on the entire graph by visiting each unvisited vertex and calling the topologicalSortUtil function, which recursively explores the neighbors of a vertex.

The main function creates an instance of the Graph class, adds directed edges, and then performs topological sort using the topologicalSort function. The sorted order is displayed as the topological sort order.

5.STACK

5.1. Implement a stack using arrays (Push and pop operations)

Below is an example of implementing a stack using arrays with push and pop operations using a class in C++:

```
#include <iostream>
class Stack {
private:
   static const int MAX_SIZE = 100;
   int arr[MAX_SIZE];
   int top;
public:
   // Constructor
   Stack() : top(-1) {}
   // Function to push an element onto the stack
   void push(int value) {
      if (top >= MAX_SIZE - 1) {
         std::cout << "Stack Overflow: Cannot push element " << value << ", the stack is full."
<< std::endl;
         return;
      }
      arr[++top] = value;
      std::cout << "Pushed element: " << value << std::endl;
   }
   // Function to pop an element from the stack
   void pop() {
      if (top < 0) {
         std::cout << "Stack Underflow: Cannot pop element, the stack is empty." << std::endl;
         return;
      }
      std::cout << "Popped element: " << arr[top--] << std::endl;
   }
   // Function to check if the stack is empty
   bool isEmpty() const {
```

```
        return (top < 0);
    }
    // Function to get the top element of the stack without popping it
    int peek() const {
        if (top < 0) {
            std::cerr << "Stack is empty." << std::endl;
            return -1; // Assuming -1 is not a valid element in the stack
        }
        return arr[top];
    }
};
int main() {
    Stack stack;
    // Push elements onto the stack
    stack.push(10);
    stack.push(20);
    stack.push(30);
    // Peek and pop elements from the stack
    std::cout << "Top element: " << stack.peek() << std::endl;
    stack.pop();
    std::cout << "Top element: " << stack.peek() << std::endl;
    // Push more elements onto the stack
    stack.push(40);
    stack.push(50);
    // Pop remaining elements from the stack
    while (!stack.isEmpty()) {
        stack.pop();
    }
    return 0;
}
```

In this example, the Stack class represents a stack implemented using an array. It includes functions for pushing elements onto the stack (push), popping elements from the stack (pop), checking if the stack is empty (isEmpty), and getting the top element without popping it (peek). The main function demonstrates the usage of the stack by pushing and popping elements.

5.2. Implement a stack using linked lists (Push and pop operations)

Below is an example of implementing a stack using linked lists with push and pop operations using a class in C++:

```
#include <iostream>
class Node {
public:
    int data;
    Node* next;
    // Constructor
    Node(int value) : data(value), next(nullptr) {}
};
class Stack {
private:
    Node* top;
public:
    // Constructor
    Stack() : top(nullptr) {}
    // Function to push an element onto the stack
    void push(int value) {
        Node* newNode = new Node(value);
        newNode->next = top;
        top = newNode;
        std::cout << "Pushed element: " << value << std::endl;
    }
    // Function to pop an element from the stack
    void pop() {
        if (isEmpty()) {
            std::cout << "Stack Underflow: Cannot pop element, the stack is empty." << std::endl;
            return;
        }
        Node* temp = top;
        top = top->next;
        std::cout << "Popped element: " << temp->data << std::endl;
```

```
        delete temp;
    }
    // Function to check if the stack is empty
    bool isEmpty() const {
        return (top == nullptr);
    }
    // Function to get the top element of the stack without popping it
    int peek() const {
        if (isEmpty()) {
            std::cerr << "Stack is empty." << std::endl;
            return -1; // Assuming -1 is not a valid element in the stack
        }
        return top->data;
    }
    // Destructor to free memory occupied by the stack
    ~Stack() {
        while (!isEmpty()) {
            pop();
        }
    }
};
int main() {
    Stack stack;
    // Push elements onto the stack
    stack.push(10);
    stack.push(20);
    stack.push(30);
    // Peek and pop elements from the stack
    std::cout << "Top element: " << stack.peek() << std::endl;
    stack.pop();
    std::cout << "Top element: " << stack.peek() << std::endl;
    // Push more elements onto the stack
    stack.push(40);
```

```
    stack.push(50);
    // Pop remaining elements from the stack
    while (!stack.isEmpty()) {
        stack.pop();
    }
    return 0;
}
```

In this example, the Stack class represents a stack implemented using a linked list. The Node class represents a node in the linked list. The Stack class includes functions for pushing elements onto the stack (push), popping elements from the stack (pop), checking if the stack is empty (isEmpty), and getting the top element without popping it (peek). The main function demonstrates the usage of the stack by pushing and popping elements. The destructor is included to free the memory occupied by the stack when the program exits.

5.3. Evaluate a post fix expression using a stack

Below is an example of implementing the evaluation of a postfix expression using a stack with a class in C++:

```
#include <iostream>
#include <stack>
#include <cctype> // For isdigit
class PostfixEvaluator {
private:
    std::stack<int> operandStack;
public:
    // Function to evaluate a postfix expression
    int evaluatePostfix(const std::string& expression) {
        for (char ch : expression) {
            if (isdigit(ch)) {
                // If the character is a digit, push it onto the operand stack
                operandStack.push(ch - '0');
            } else if (ch == '+' || ch == '-' || ch == '*' || ch == '/') {
                // If the character is an operator, pop two operands, perform the operation, and push
the result
                if (operandStack.size() < 2) {
                    std::cerr << "Error: Insufficient operands for operator " << ch << std::endl;
                    return -1; // Error condition
                }
                int operand2 = operandStack.top();
                operandStack.pop();
                int operand1 = operandStack.top();
                operandStack.pop();
                switch (ch) {
                    case '+':
                        operandStack.push(operand1 + operand2);
                        break;
                    case '-':
                        operandStack.push(operand1 - operand2);
```

```
                    break;
                case '*':
                    operandStack.push(operand1 * operand2);
                    break;
                case '/':
                    if (operand2 == 0) {
                        std::cerr << "Error: Division by zero" << std::endl;
                        return -1; // Error condition
                    }
                    operandStack.push(operand1 / operand2);
                    break;
                default:
                    std::cerr << "Error: Invalid operator " << ch << std::endl;
                    return -1; // Error condition
            }
        }
    }
    // The result should be the only element left on the stack
    if (operandStack.size() == 1) {
        return operandStack.top();
    } else {
        std::cerr << "Error: Invalid postfix expression" << std::endl;
        return -1; // Error condition
    }
  }
};
int main() {
  PostfixEvaluator postfixEvaluator;
  // Example postfix expressions
  std::string expression1 = "23*5+";
  std::string expression2 = "82/3-";
  std::string expression3 = "42*8/";
  // Evaluate expressions
```

```
    int result1 = postfixEvaluator.evaluatePostfix(expression1);
    int result2 = postfixEvaluator.evaluatePostfix(expression2);
    int result3 = postfixEvaluator.evaluatePostfix(expression3);
    // Display results
    std::cout << "Result of " << expression1 << ": " << result1 << std::endl;
    std::cout << "Result of " << expression2 << ": " << result2 << std::endl;
    std::cout << "Result of " << expression3 << ": " << result3 << std::endl;
    return 0;
}
```

In this example, the PostfixEvaluator class encapsulates the logic for evaluating a postfix expression. The evaluatePostfix function takes a postfix expression as input and uses a stack (operandStack) to perform the evaluation. The main function demonstrates how to use the PostfixEvaluator class to evaluate different postfix expressions.

5.4. Use a stack to check for balanced parentheses in an expression

Below is an example of implementing a balanced parentheses checker using a stack with a class in C++:

```
#include <iostream>
#include <stack>
class BalancedParenthesesChecker {
private:
  std::stack<char> charStack;
public:
  // Function to check for balanced parentheses in an expression
  bool checkBalancedParentheses(const std::string& expression) {
    for (char ch : expression) {
      if (ch == '(' || ch == '[' || ch == '{') {
        // If the character is an opening parenthesis, push it onto the stack
        charStack.push(ch);
      } else if (ch == ')' || ch == ']' || ch == '}') {
        // If the character is a closing parenthesis, check for a matching opening parenthesis
        if (charStack.empty()) {
          return false; // Unmatched closing parenthesis
        }
        char topChar = charStack.top();
        charStack.pop();
        if ((ch == ')' && topChar != '(') ||
          (ch == ']' && topChar != '[') ||
          (ch == '}' && topChar != '{')) {
          return false; // Mismatched opening parenthesis
        }
      }
    }
    // Check if there are any remaining unmatched opening parentheses
    return charStack.empty();
  }
};
```

```
int main() {
    BalancedParenthesesChecker parenthesesChecker;
    // Example expressions
    std::string expression1 = "{(a+b)*[c-d]}";
    std::string expression2 = "([a+b]*c)-d}";
    // Check for balanced parentheses
    bool isBalanced1 = parenthesesChecker.checkBalancedParentheses(expression1);
    bool isBalanced2 = parenthesesChecker.checkBalancedParentheses(expression2);
    // Display results
    std::cout << "Expression 1 is " << (isBalanced1 ? "balanced" : "not balanced") <<
std::endl;
    std::cout << "Expression 2 is " << (isBalanced2 ? "balanced" : "not balanced") <<
std::endl;

    return 0;
}
```

In this example, the BalancedParenthesesChecker class encapsulates the logic for checking balanced parentheses in an expression. The checkBalancedParentheses function takes an expression as input and uses a stack (charStack) to keep track of opening parentheses. When a closing parenthesis is encountered, it checks for a matching opening parenthesis on the stack.

The main function demonstrates how to use the BalancedParenthesesChecker class to check for balanced parentheses in two example expressions. The results are displayed indicating whether each expression is balanced or not.

6.QUEUE

6.1. Implement a queue using arrays (enqueue and dequeue operations)

Below is an example of implementing a queue using arrays with enqueue and dequeue operations using a class in C++:

```
#include <iostream>
class Queue {
private:
    static const int MAX_SIZE = 100;
    int arr[MAX_SIZE];
    int front, rear;
public:
    // Constructor
    Queue() : front(-1), rear(-1) {}
    // Function to check if the queue is empty
    bool isEmpty() const {
        return (front == -1 && rear == -1);
    }
    // Function to check if the queue is full
    bool isFull() const {
        return (rear == MAX_SIZE - 1);
    }
    // Function to enqueue (insert) an element into the queue
    void enqueue(int value) {
        if (isFull()) {
            std::cout << "Queue Overflow: Cannot enqueue element " << value << ", the queue is full." << std::endl;
            return;
        }
        if (isEmpty()) {
            front = 0; // Set front to 0 when enqueueing the first element
        }
        arr[++rear] = value;
        std::cout << "Enqueued element: " << value << std::endl;
```

```
    }
    // Function to dequeue (remove) an element from the queue
    void dequeue() {
        if (isEmpty()) {
            std::cout << "Queue Underflow: Cannot dequeue element, the queue is empty." <<
std::endl;
            return;
        }
        std::cout << "Dequeued element: " << arr[front++] << std::endl;
        // Reset front and rear when the last element is dequeued
        if (front > rear) {
            front = rear = -1;
        }
    }
    // Function to get the front element of the queue without dequeuing it
    int peek() const {
        if (isEmpty()) {
            std::cerr << "Queue is empty." << std::endl;
            return -1; // Assuming -1 is not a valid element in the queue
        }
        return arr[front];
    }
};
int main() {
    Queue queue;
    // Enqueue elements into the queue
    queue.enqueue(10);
    queue.enqueue(20);
    queue.enqueue(30);
    // Peek and dequeue elements from the queue
    std::cout << "Front element: " << queue.peek() << std::endl;
    queue.dequeue();
    std::cout << "Front element: " << queue.peek() << std::endl;
```

```
    // Enqueue more elements into the queue
    queue.enqueue(40);
    queue.enqueue(50);
    // Dequeue remaining elements from the queue
    while (!queue.isEmpty()) {
        queue.dequeue();
    }
    return 0;
}
```

In this example, the Queue class represents a queue implemented using an array. It includes functions for checking if the queue is empty (isEmpty), checking if the queue is full (isFull), enqueuing elements into the queue (enqueue), dequeuing elements from the queue (dequeue), and getting the front element without dequeuing it (peek). The main function demonstrates the usage of the queue by enqueuing and dequeuing elements.

6.2. Implement a queue using linked lists (enqueue and dequeue operations)

Below is an example of implementing a queue using linked lists with enqueue and dequeue operations using a class in C++:

```
#include <iostream>
class Node {
public:
    int data;
    Node* next;
    // Constructor
    Node(int value) : data(value), next(nullptr) {}
};
class Queue {
private:
    Node* front;
    Node* rear;
public:
    // Constructor
    Queue() : front(nullptr), rear(nullptr) {}
    // Function to check if the queue is empty
    bool isEmpty() const {
        return (front == nullptr);
    }
    // Function to enqueue (insert) an element into the queue
    void enqueue(int value) {
        Node* newNode = new Node(value);
        if (isEmpty()) {
            front = rear = newNode;
        } else {
            rear->next = newNode;
            rear = newNode;
        }
        std::cout << "Enqueued element: " << value << std::endl;
    }
```

```
    // Function to dequeue (remove) an element from the queue
    void dequeue() {
        if (isEmpty()) {
            std::cout << "Queue Underflow: Cannot dequeue element, the queue is empty." <<
std::endl;
            return;
        }
        Node* temp = front;
        front = front->next;
        std::cout << "Dequeued element: " << temp->data << std::endl;

        delete temp;

        // Reset rear when the last element is dequeued
        if (front == nullptr) {
            rear = nullptr;
        }
    }
    // Function to get the front element of the queue without dequeuing it
    int peek() const {
        if (isEmpty()) {
            std::cerr << "Queue is empty." << std::endl;
            return -1; // Assuming -1 is not a valid element in the queue
        }
        return front->data;
    }
    // Destructor to free memory occupied by the queue
    ~Queue() {
        while (!isEmpty()) {
            dequeue();
        }
    }
};
```

```
int main() {
    Queue queue;
    // Enqueue elements into the queue
    queue.enqueue(10);
    queue.enqueue(20);
    queue.enqueue(30);
    // Peek and dequeue elements from the queue
    std::cout << "Front element: " << queue.peek() << std::endl;
    queue.dequeue();
    std::cout << "Front element: " << queue.peek() << std::endl;
    // Enqueue more elements into the queue
    queue.enqueue(40);
    queue.enqueue(50);
    // Dequeue remaining elements from the queue
    while (!queue.isEmpty()) {
        queue.dequeue();
    }
    return 0;
}
```

In this example, the Queue class represents a queue implemented using a linked list. The Node class represents a node in the linked list. The Queue class includes functions for checking if the queue is empty (isEmpty), enqueuing elements into the queue (enqueue), dequeuing elements from the queue (dequeue), and getting the front element without dequeuing it (peek). The main function demonstrates the usage of the queue by enqueuing and dequeuing elements. The destructor is included to free the memory occupied by the queue when the program exits.

6.3. Circular queue implementation (enqueue and dequeue operations)

Below is an example of implementing a circular queue using arrays with enqueue and dequeue operations using a class in C++:

```
#include <iostream>
class CircularQueue {
private:
    static const int MAX_SIZE = 5;  // Maximum size of the circular queue
    int arr[MAX_SIZE];
    int front, rear;
public:
    // Constructor
    CircularQueue() : front(-1), rear(-1) {}
    // Function to check if the circular queue is empty
    bool isEmpty() const {
        return (front == -1 && rear == -1);
    }
    // Function to check if the circular queue is full
    bool isFull() const {
        return ((rear + 1) % MAX_SIZE == front);
    }
    // Function to enqueue (insert) an element into the circular queue
    void enqueue(int value) {
        if (isFull()) {
            std::cout << "Circular Queue Overflow: Cannot enqueue element " << value << ", the
queue is full." << std::endl;
            return;
        }
        if (isEmpty()) {
            front = rear = 0;
        } else {
            rear = (rear + 1) % MAX_SIZE;
        }
        arr[rear] = value;
```

```
        std::cout << "Enqueued element: " << value << std::endl;
    }
    // Function to dequeue (remove) an element from the circular queue
    void dequeue() {
        if (isEmpty()) {
            std::cout << "Circular Queue Underflow: Cannot dequeue element, the queue is
empty." << std::endl;
            return;
        }
        std::cout << "Dequeued element: " << arr[front] << std::endl;
        if (front == rear) {
            // Reset front and rear when the last element is dequeued
            front = rear = -1;
        } else {
            front = (front + 1) % MAX_SIZE;
        }
    }
    // Function to display the circular queue
    void display() const {
        if (isEmpty()) {
            std::cout << "Circular Queue is empty." << std::endl;
            return;
        }
        int i = front;
        do {
            std::cout << arr[i] << " ";
            i = (i + 1) % MAX_SIZE;
        } while (i != (rear + 1) % MAX_SIZE);
        std::cout << std::endl;
    }
};
int main() {
    CircularQueue circularQueue;
```

```
    // Enqueue elements into the circular queue
    circularQueue.enqueue(10);
    circularQueue.enqueue(20);
    circularQueue.enqueue(30);
    // Display the circular queue
    std::cout << "Circular Queue after enqueue operations: ";
    circularQueue.display();
    // Dequeue elements from the circular queue
    circularQueue.dequeue();
    circularQueue.dequeue();
    // Display the circular queue
    std::cout << "Circular Queue after dequeue operations: ";
    circularQueue.display();
    // Enqueue more elements into the circular queue
    circularQueue.enqueue(40);
    circularQueue.enqueue(50);
    // Display the circular queue
    std::cout << "Circular Queue after additional enqueue operations: ";
    circularQueue.display();
    return 0;
}
```

In this example, the CircularQueue class represents a circular queue implemented using an array. The CircularQueue class includes functions for checking if the circular queue is empty (isEmpty), checking if the circular queue is full (isFull), enqueuing elements into the circular queue (enqueue), dequeuing elements from the circular queue (dequeue), and displaying the circular queue (display). The main function demonstrates the usage of the circular queue by performing enqueue and dequeue operations.

6.4. Simulate a real-world scenario using a queue (Ex. Print queue)

Let's simulate a print queue scenario using a queue implemented with a class in C++. In this scenario, we'll consider a simple print queue for a printer where print jobs are added to the queue and processed in a first-come-first-serve manner.

```
#include <iostream>
#include <queue>
#include <string>
class PrintQueue {
private:
    std::queue<std::string> jobQueue;
public:
    // Function to add a print job to the queue
    void enqueueJob(const std::string& job) {
        jobQueue.push(job);
        std::cout << "Added print job: " << job << " to the queue." << std::endl;
    }
    // Function to process the next print job in the queue
    void processNextJob() {
        if (!jobQueue.empty()) {
            std::string job = jobQueue.front();
            jobQueue.pop();
            std::cout << "Processing print job: " << job << std::endl;
        } else {
            std::cout << "Print queue is empty. No job to process." << std::endl;
        }
    }
    // Function to display the current print queue
    void displayQueue() const {
        if (jobQueue.empty()) {
            std::cout << "Print queue is empty." << std::endl;
        } else {
            std::cout << "Current Print Queue: ";
            std::queue<std::string> tempQueue = jobQueue;
```

```
            while (!tempQueue.empty()) {
                std::cout << tempQueue.front() << " ";
                tempQueue.pop();
            }
            std::cout << std::endl;
        }
    }
};
int main() {
    PrintQueue printer;
    // Enqueue print jobs
    printer.enqueueJob("Document1");
    printer.enqueueJob("Document2");
    printer.enqueueJob("Document3");
    // Display the current print queue
    printer.displayQueue();
    // Process print jobs
    printer.processNextJob();
    printer.processNextJob();
    // Display the updated print queue
    printer.displayQueue();
    // Enqueue more print jobs
    printer.enqueueJob("Document4");
    printer.enqueueJob("Document5");
    // Display the final print queue
    printer.displayQueue();

    return 0;
}
```

In this example, the PrintQueue class represents a print queue. The class includes functions for enqueuing print jobs (enqueueJob), processing the next print job (processNextJob), and displaying the current print queue (displayQueue). The main function demonstrates the usage of the print queue by enqueuing print jobs, processing them, and displaying the updated print queue.

7. TREE

7.1. Binary tree traversal (In-order, Pre-order and Post-order)

Below is an example of implementing binary tree traversal (in-order, pre-order, and post-order) using a class in C++:

```
#include <iostream>
class Node {
public:
  int data;
  Node* left;
  Node* right;
  // Constructor
  Node(int value) : data(value), left(nullptr), right(nullptr) {}
};
class BinaryTree {
private:
  Node* root;
  // Helper function for in-order traversal
  void inOrderTraversalHelper(Node* node) {
    if (node) {
      inOrderTraversalHelper(node->left);
      std::cout << node->data << " ";
      inOrderTraversalHelper(node->right);
    }
  }
  // Helper function for pre-order traversal
  void preOrderTraversalHelper(Node* node) {
    if (node) {
      std::cout << node->data << " ";
      preOrderTraversalHelper(node->left);
      preOrderTraversalHelper(node->right);
    }
  }
  // Helper function for post-order traversal
```

```
    void postOrderTraversalHelper(Node* node) {
        if (node) {
            postOrderTraversalHelper(node->left);
            postOrderTraversalHelper(node->right);
            std::cout << node->data << " ";
        }
    }
public:
    // Constructor
    BinaryTree() : root(nullptr) {}
    // Function to insert a node into the binary tree
    Node* insertNode(int value) {
        return insertNodeHelper(root, value);
    }
    // Helper function for node insertion
    Node* insertNodeHelper(Node* currentNode, int value) {
        if (currentNode == nullptr) {
            return new Node(value);
        }
        if (value < currentNode->data) {
            currentNode->left = insertNodeHelper(currentNode->left, value);
        } else if (value > currentNode->data) {
            currentNode->right = insertNodeHelper(currentNode->right, value);
        }
        return currentNode;
    }
    // Function to perform in-order traversal
    void inOrderTraversal() {
        std::cout << "In-order Traversal: ";
        inOrderTraversalHelper(root);
        std::cout << std::endl;
    }
    // Function to perform pre-order traversal
```

```
    void preOrderTraversal() {
        std::cout << "Pre-order Traversal: ";
        preOrderTraversalHelper(root);
        std::cout << std::endl;
    }
    // Function to perform post-order traversal
    void postOrderTraversal() {
        std::cout << "Post-order Traversal: ";
        postOrderTraversalHelper(root);
        std::cout << std::endl;
    }
};
int main() {
    BinaryTree binaryTree;
    // Insert nodes into the binary tree
    binaryTree.insertNode(50);
    binaryTree.insertNode(30);
    binaryTree.insertNode(70);
    binaryTree.insertNode(20);
    binaryTree.insertNode(40);
    binaryTree.insertNode(60);
    binaryTree.insertNode(80);
    // Perform different tree traversals
    binaryTree.inOrderTraversal();
    binaryTree.preOrderTraversal();
    binaryTree.postOrderTraversal();
    return 0;
}
```

In this example, the BinaryTree class represents a binary tree. The Node class represents a node in the binary tree. The BinaryTree class includes functions for inserting a node into the binary tree (insertNode) and performing in-order, pre-order, and post-order traversals (inOrderTraversal, preOrderTraversal, postOrderTraversal). The main function demonstrates the usage of the binary tree by inserting nodes and performing different tree traversals.

7.2. Find the height of a binary tree.

Below is an example of finding the height of a binary tree using a class in C++:

```
#include <iostream>
#include <algorithm> // For std::max
class Node {
public:
    int data;
    Node* left;
    Node* right;
    // Constructor
    Node(int value) : data(value), left(nullptr), right(nullptr) {}
};
class BinaryTree {
private:
    Node* root;
    // Helper function for finding the height of a binary tree
    int heightHelper(Node* node) {
        if (node == nullptr) {
            return 0;
        }
        // Recursively calculate the height of the left and right subtrees
        int leftHeight = heightHelper(node->left);
        int rightHeight = heightHelper(node->right);
        // Return the maximum height of the left and right subtrees, plus 1 for the current node
        return 1 + std::max(leftHeight, rightHeight);
    }
public:
    // Constructor
    BinaryTree() : root(nullptr) {}
    // Function to insert a node into the binary tree
    Node* insertNode(int value) {
        return insertNodeHelper(root, value);
    }
```

```
    // Helper function for node insertion
    Node* insertNodeHelper(Node* currentNode, int value) {
        if (currentNode == nullptr) {
            return new Node(value);
        }
        if (value < currentNode->data) {
            currentNode->left = insertNodeHelper(currentNode->left, value);
        } else if (value > currentNode->data) {
            currentNode->right = insertNodeHelper(currentNode->right, value);
        }
        return currentNode;
    }
    // Function to find the height of the binary tree
    int height() {
        return heightHelper(root);
    }
};
int main() {
    BinaryTree binaryTree;
    // Insert nodes into the binary tree
    binaryTree.insertNode(50);
    binaryTree.insertNode(30);
    binaryTree.insertNode(70);
    binaryTree.insertNode(20);
    binaryTree.insertNode(40);
    binaryTree.insertNode(60);
    binaryTree.insertNode(80);
    // Find and display the height of the binary tree
    int treeHeight = binaryTree.height();
    std::cout << "Height of the binary tree: " << treeHeight << std::endl;
    return 0;
}
```

In this example, the BinaryTree class represents a binary tree. The Node class represents a node in the binary tree. The BinaryTree class includes a helper function (heightHelper) for finding the height of a binary tree, and the public function height uses this helper function to calculate the height of the entire tree. The main function demonstrates the usage of the binary tree by inserting nodes and finding the height of the tree.

7.3. Binary Search tree insert, delete, display and search operations

Below is an example of implementing binary search tree operations (insert, delete, display, and search) using a class in C++:

```
#include <iostream>
class Node {
public:
    int data;
    Node* left;
    Node* right;
    // Constructor
    Node(int value) : data(value), left(nullptr), right(nullptr) {}
};
class BinarySearchTree {
private:
    Node* root;
    // Helper function for inserting a node into the binary search tree
    Node* insertNodeHelper(Node* currentNode, int value) {
        if (currentNode == nullptr) {
            return new Node(value);
        }
        if (value < currentNode->data) {
            currentNode->left = insertNodeHelper(currentNode->left, value);
        } else if (value > currentNode->data) {
            currentNode->right = insertNodeHelper(currentNode->right, value);
        }
        return currentNode;
    }
    // Helper function for finding the minimum value node in a binary search tree
    Node* findMinValueNode(Node* node) {
        Node* current = node;
        while (current->left != nullptr) {
            current = current->left;
        }
```

```
        return current;
    }
    // Helper function for deleting a node with a given value from the binary search tree
    Node* deleteNodeHelper(Node* currentNode, int value) {
        if (currentNode == nullptr) {
            return nullptr;
        }
        if (value < currentNode->data) {
            currentNode->left = deleteNodeHelper(currentNode->left, value);
        } else if (value > currentNode->data) {
            currentNode->right = deleteNodeHelper(currentNode->right, value);
        } else {
            // Node with only one child or no child
            if (currentNode->left == nullptr) {
                Node* temp = currentNode->right;
                delete currentNode;
                return temp;
            } else if (currentNode->right == nullptr) {
                Node* temp = currentNode->left;
                delete currentNode;
                return temp;
            }
            // Node with two children: Get the inorder successor (smallest in the right subtree)
            Node* temp = findMinValueNode(currentNode->right);
            // Copy the inorder successor's data to this node
            currentNode->data = temp->data;
            // Delete the inorder successor
            currentNode->right = deleteNodeHelper(currentNode->right, temp->data);
        }
        return currentNode;
    }
    // Helper function for in-order traversal to display the tree
    void displayTreeHelper(Node* node) {
```

```
        if (node) {
            displayTreeHelper(node->left);
            std::cout << node->data << " ";
            displayTreeHelper(node->right);
        }
    }
    // Helper function for searching a value in the binary search tree
    bool searchValueHelper(Node* node, int value) {
        if (node == nullptr) {
            return false;
        }
        if (value == node->data) {
            return true;
        } else if (value < node->data) {
            return searchValueHelper(node->left, value);
        } else {
            return searchValueHelper(node->right, value);
        }
    }
public:
    // Constructor
    BinarySearchTree() : root(nullptr) {}

    // Function to insert a node into the binary search tree
    void insertNode(int value) {
        root = insertNodeHelper(root, value);
    }
    // Function to delete a node with a given value from the binary search tree
    void deleteNode(int value) {
        root = deleteNodeHelper(root, value);
    }
    // Function to display the binary search tree
    void displayTree() {
```

```
        std::cout << "Binary Search Tree: ";
        displayTreeHelper(root);
        std::cout << std::endl;
    }
    // Function to search for a value in the binary search tree
    bool searchValue(int value) {
        return searchValueHelper(root, value);
    }
};
int main() {
    BinarySearchTree bst;
    // Insert nodes into the binary search tree
    bst.insertNode(50);
    bst.insertNode(30);
    bst.insertNode(70);
    bst.insertNode(20);
    bst.insertNode(40);
    bst.insertNode(60);
    bst.insertNode(80);
    // Display the binary search tree
    bst.displayTree();

    // Search for values in the binary search tree
    int searchValue1 = 40;
    int searchValue2 = 90;
    std::cout << "Search for value " << searchValue1 << ": " <<
(bst.searchValue(searchValue1) ? "Found" : "Not Found") << std::endl;
    std::cout << "Search for value " << searchValue2 << ": " <<
(bst.searchValue(searchValue2) ? "Found" : "Not Found") << std::endl;
    // Delete a node from the binary search tree
    int deleteValue = 30;
    bst.deleteNode(deleteValue);
    // Display the updated binary search tree
```

```
  bst.displayTree();
  return 0;
}
```

In this example, the BinarySearchTree class represents a binary search tree. The Node class represents a node in the binary search tree. The BinarySearchTree class includes functions for inserting a node into the binary search tree (insertNode), deleting a node with a given value from the binary search tree (deleteNode), displaying the binary search tree (displayTree), and searching for a value in the binary search tree (searchValue). The main function demonstrates the usage of the binary search tree by inserting nodes, displaying the tree, searching for values, and deleting a node.

7.4.AVL tree (or) Red-black tree implementation

Implementing a full AVL tree or Red-Black tree involves complex balancing and rotation operations, and it would be a more extensive piece of code. However, I can provide you with a simple example of an AVL tree implementation using a class in C++. Keep in mind that a complete AVL tree implementation requires careful balancing after insertions and deletions, and the code may become more complex. Here's a basic example of an AVL tree implementation with insertion:

```
#include <iostream>
class Node {
public:
   int data;
   Node* left;
   Node* right;
   int height;
   Node(int value) : data(value), left(nullptr), right(nullptr), height(1) {}
};
class AVLTree {
private:
   Node* root;
   int height(Node* node) {
      if (node == nullptr) {
         return 0;
      }
      return node->height;
   }
   int balanceFactor(Node* node) {
      if (node == nullptr) {
         return 0;
      }
      return height(node->left) - height(node->right);
   }
   Node* rightRotate(Node* y) {
      Node* x = y->left;
```

```
    Node* T2 = x->right;
    x->right = y;
    y->left = T2;
    y->height = std::max(height(y->left), height(y->right)) + 1;
    x->height = std::max(height(x->left), height(x->right)) + 1;
    return x;
}
Node* leftRotate(Node* x) {
    Node* y = x->right;
    Node* T2 = y->left;
    y->left = x;
    x->right = T2;
    x->height = std::max(height(x->left), height(x->right)) + 1;
    y->height = std::max(height(y->left), height(y->right)) + 1;
    return y;
}
Node* insertNodeHelper(Node* node, int value) {
    if (node == nullptr) {
        return new Node(value);
    }
    if (value < node->data) {
        node->left = insertNodeHelper(node->left, value);
    } else if (value > node->data) {
        node->right = insertNodeHelper(node->right, value);
    } else {
        // Duplicate values are not allowed
        return node;
    }
    // Update height of the current node
    node->height = 1 + std::max(height(node->left), height(node->right));
    // Perform rotations to balance the tree
    int balance = balanceFactor(node);
    // Left Left Case
```

```
        if (balance > 1 && value < node->left->data) {
            return rightRotate(node);
        }
        // Right Right Case
        if (balance < -1 && value > node->right->data) {
            return leftRotate(node);
        }
        // Left Right Case
        if (balance > 1 && value > node->left->data) {
            node->left = leftRotate(node->left);
            return rightRotate(node);
        }
        // Right Left Case
        if (balance < -1 && value < node->right->data) {
            node->right = rightRotate(node->right);
            return leftRotate(node);
        }
        return node;
    }
public:
    AVLTree() : root(nullptr) {}
    void insertNode(int value) {
        root = insertNodeHelper(root, value);
    }
    // Display the tree using in-order traversal
    void displayTree(Node* node) {
        if (node) {
            displayTree(node->left);
            std::cout << node->data << " ";
            displayTree(node->right);
        }
    }
    void displayTree() {
```

```
        std::cout << "AVL Tree (In-order traversal): ";
        displayTree(root);
        std::cout << std::endl;
    }
};
int main() {
    AVLTree avlTree;
    // Insert nodes into the AVL tree
    avlTree.insertNode(30);
    avlTree.insertNode(20);
    avlTree.insertNode(40);
    avlTree.insertNode(10);
    avlTree.insertNode(25);
    // Display the AVL tree
    avlTree.displayTree();
    return 0;
}
```

This example includes the basic operations for inserting nodes into an AVL tree and displays the tree using an in-order traversal. A complete AVL tree implementation would also involve deletion and more complex balancing cases. Similarly, a Red-Black tree implementation would have its own set of rules for maintaining balance. If you need a more comprehensive implementation, consider using existing libraries or more extensive examples available online.

7.5. Check if a binary tree is balanced

You can check if a binary tree is balanced by calculating the height difference between the left and right subtrees of each node. If the difference is greater than 1 at any node, the tree is not balanced. Below is an example of checking if a binary tree is balanced using a class in C++:

```
#include <iostream>
#include <algorithm> // For std::max
class Node {
public:
  int data;
  Node* left;
  Node* right;
  // Constructor
  Node(int value) : data(value), left(nullptr), right(nullptr) {}
};
class BinaryTree {
private:
  Node* root;
  // Helper function for checking if a binary tree is balanced
  bool isBalancedHelper(Node* node, int& height) {
    if (node == nullptr) {
      height = 0;
      return true;
    }
    int leftHeight = 0, rightHeight = 0;
    bool leftBalanced = isBalancedHelper(node->left, leftHeight);
    bool rightBalanced = isBalancedHelper(node->right, rightHeight);
    height = 1 + std::max(leftHeight, rightHeight);
    // Check if the current node is balanced
    if (std::abs(leftHeight - rightHeight) > 1) {
      return false;
    }
    // Check if both subtrees are balanced
```

```
        return leftBalanced && rightBalanced;
    }
public:
    // Constructor
    BinaryTree() : root(nullptr) {}
    // Function to insert a node into the binary tree
    Node* insertNode(int value) {
        return insertNodeHelper(root, value);
    }
    // Helper function for node insertion
    Node* insertNodeHelper(Node* currentNode, int value) {
        if (currentNode == nullptr) {
            return new Node(value);
        }
        if (value < currentNode->data) {
            currentNode->left = insertNodeHelper(currentNode->left, value);
        } else if (value > currentNode->data) {
            currentNode->right = insertNodeHelper(currentNode->right, value);
        }
        return currentNode;
    }
    // Function to check if the binary tree is balanced
    bool isBalanced() {
        int height = 0;
        return isBalancedHelper(root, height);
    }
};
int main() {
    BinaryTree binaryTree;
    // Insert nodes into the binary tree
    binaryTree.insertNode(50);
    binaryTree.insertNode(30);
    binaryTree.insertNode(70);
```

```
    binaryTree.insertNode(20);
    binaryTree.insertNode(40);
    binaryTree.insertNode(60);
    binaryTree.insertNode(80);
    // Check if the binary tree is balanced
    bool balanced = binaryTree.isBalanced();
    if (balanced) {
        std::cout << "The binary tree is balanced." << std::endl;
    } else {
        std::cout << "The binary tree is not balanced." << std::endl;
    }
    return 0;
}
```

In this example, the BinaryTree class includes a helper function (isBalancedHelper) that checks whether a given binary tree is balanced or not. The function returns a boolean value indicating the balance status and calculates the height of the subtree rooted at the current node. The main function demonstrates the usage of this functionality by creating a binary tree and checking if it is balanced.

7.6.Convert a binary search tree to a doubly linked list

It provide you with a simple C++ implementation for converting a Binary Search Tree (BST) to a doubly linked list (DLL). In this example, I'll use a class to represent the nodes of the BST and DLL.

```
#include <iostream>
class Node {
public:
    int data;
    Node* left;
    Node* right;
    // Constructor
    Node(int value) : data(value), left(nullptr), right(nullptr) {}
};
class BSTToDLLConverter {
private:
    Node* root;
    Node* prev; // Keep track of the previously visited node
    // Helper function to perform in-order traversal and convert BST to DLL
    void convertToDLLHelper(Node* node) {
        if (node == nullptr) {
            return;
        }
        // Recursively convert the left subtree
        convertToDLLHelper(node->left);
        // Modify the tree structure to form the doubly linked list
        if (prev == nullptr) {
            // If prev is null, it means this is the first node (leftmost node)
            root = node;
        } else {
            // Link the previous node's right to the current node
            prev->right = node;
            // Link the current node's left to the previous node
            node->left = prev;
```

```
        }
        // Update prev to the current node
        prev = node;
        // Recursively convert the right subtree
        convertToDLLHelper(node->right);
    }
public:
    // Constructor
    BSTToDLLConverter() : root(nullptr), prev(nullptr) {}
    // Function to insert a node into the BST
    Node* insertNode(int value) {
        return insertNodeHelper(root, value);
    }
    // Helper function for node insertion
    Node* insertNodeHelper(Node* currentNode, int value) {
        if (currentNode == nullptr) {
            return new Node(value);
        }
        if (value < currentNode->data) {
            currentNode->left = insertNodeHelper(currentNode->left, value);
        } else if (value > currentNode->data) {
            currentNode->right = insertNodeHelper(currentNode->right, value);
        }
        return currentNode;
    }
    // Function to convert BST to DLL
    Node* convertToDLL() {
        convertToDLLHelper(root);
        return root;
    }
};
// Function to display the doubly linked list
void displayDLL(Node* head) {
```

```
    std::cout << "Doubly Linked List: ";
    while (head != nullptr) {
        std::cout << head->data << " ";
        head = head->right;
    }
    std::cout << std::endl;
}
int main() {
    BSTToDLLConverter bstToDLLConverter;
    // Insert nodes into the BST
    bstToDLLConverter.insertNode(50);
    bstToDLLConverter.insertNode(30);
    bstToDLLConverter.insertNode(70);
    bstToDLLConverter.insertNode(20);
    bstToDLLConverter.insertNode(40);
    bstToDLLConverter.insertNode(60);
    bstToDLLConverter.insertNode(80);
    // Convert BST to DLL
    Node* head = bstToDLLConverter.convertToDLL();
    // Display the doubly linked list
    displayDLL(head);
    return 0;
}
```

In this example, the BSTToDLLConverter class has a member function convertToDLL() that initiates the conversion process, and the actual conversion is done by the helper function convertToDLLHelper(). The doubly linked list is then displayed using the displayDLL() function.

8.GRAPHS

8.1. Implement an adjacency matrix

Below is an example of implementing an adjacency matrix using a class in C++. In this example, I'm assuming an undirected graph.

```
#include <iostream>
#include <vector>
class Graph {
private:
    int numVertices;
    std::vector<std::vector<int>> adjacencyMatrix;
public:
    // Constructor
    Graph(int vertices) : numVertices(vertices), adjacencyMatrix(vertices,
std::vector<int>(vertices, 0)) {}
    // Function to add an edge to the graph
    void addEdge(int source, int destination) {
        if (source >= 0 && source < numVertices && destination >= 0 && destination <
numVertices) {
            // For an undirected graph, set both source to destination and destination to source
            adjacencyMatrix[source][destination] = 1;
            adjacencyMatrix[destination][source] = 1;
        } else {
            std::cerr << "Invalid vertices for edge addition." << std::endl;
        }
    }
    // Function to display the adjacency matrix
    void displayMatrix() const {
        std::cout << "Adjacency Matrix:" << std::endl;
        for (int i = 0; i < numVertices; ++i) {
            for (int j = 0; j < numVertices; ++j) {
                std::cout << adjacencyMatrix[i][j] << " ";
            }
            std::cout << std::endl;
```

```
        }
    }
};
int main() {
    // Create a graph with 5 vertices
    Graph graph(5);
    // Add edges to the graph
    graph.addEdge(0, 1);
    graph.addEdge(0, 4);
    graph.addEdge(1, 2);
    graph.addEdge(1, 3);
    graph.addEdge(1, 4);
    graph.addEdge(2, 3);
    graph.addEdge(3, 4);
    // Display the adjacency matrix
    graph.displayMatrix();
    return 0;
}
```

In this example, the Graph class has a member variable adjacencyMatrix, which is a 2D vector representing the adjacency matrix. The addEdge function is used to add an edge to the graph, and the displayMatrix function is used to display the adjacency matrix.

This example assumes an undirected graph, where adding an edge from vertex A to vertex B is the same as adding an edge from vertex B to vertex A. Adjustments may be needed if you are working with a directed graph.

8.2. Implement an adjacency list

Below is an example of implementing an adjacency list using a class in C++. This example assumes an undirected graph.

```
#include <iostream>
#include <list>
#include <vector>
class Graph {
private:
    int numVertices;
    std::vector<std::list<int>> adjacencyList;
public:
    // Constructor
    Graph(int vertices) : numVertices(vertices), adjacencyList(vertices) {}
    // Function to add an edge to the graph
    void addEdge(int source, int destination) {
        if (source >= 0 && source < numVertices && destination >= 0 && destination <
numVertices) {
            // For an undirected graph, add destination to the source's adjacency list and vice versa
            adjacencyList[source].push_back(destination);
            adjacencyList[destination].push_back(source);
        } else {
            std::cerr << "Invalid vertices for edge addition." << std::endl;
        }
    }
    // Function to display the adjacency list
    void displayList() const {
        std::cout << "Adjacency List:" << std::endl;
        for (int i = 0; i < numVertices; ++i) {
            std::cout << "Vertex " << i << ": ";
            for (const auto& neighbor : adjacencyList[i]) {
                std::cout << neighbor << " ";
            }
            std::cout << std::endl;
```

```
        }
    }
};
int main() {
    // Create a graph with 5 vertices
    Graph graph(5);
    // Add edges to the graph
    graph.addEdge(0, 1);
    graph.addEdge(0, 4);
    graph.addEdge(1, 2);
    graph.addEdge(1, 3);
    graph.addEdge(1, 4);
    graph.addEdge(2, 3);
    graph.addEdge(3, 4);
    // Display the adjacency list
    graph.displayList();
    return 0;
}
```

In this example, the Graph class has a member variable adjacencyList, which is a vector of lists representing the adjacency list. The addEdge function is used to add an edge to the graph, and the displayList function is used to display the adjacency list.

This example assumes an undirected graph, where adding an edge from vertex A to vertex B is the same as adding an edge from vertex B to vertex A. Adjustments may be needed if you are working with a directed graph.

8.3.DFS

Below is an example of Depth-First Search (DFS) implemented using a class in C++. In this example, the graph is represented using an adjacency list.

```
#include <iostream>
#include <list>
#include <vector>
#include <stack>
class Graph {
private:
    int numVertices;
    std::vector<std::list<int>> adjacencyList;
public:
    // Constructor
    Graph(int vertices) : numVertices(vertices), adjacencyList(vertices) {}
    // Function to add an edge to the graph
    void addEdge(int source, int destination) {
        if (source >= 0 && source < numVertices && destination >= 0 && destination <
numVertices) {
            adjacencyList[source].push_back(destination);
        } else {
            std::cerr << "Invalid vertices for edge addition." << std::endl;
        }
    }
    // Function to perform Depth-First Search
    void DFS(int startVertex) {
        // Vector to keep track of visited vertices
        std::vector<bool> visited(numVertices, false);
        // Stack for DFS traversal
        std::stack<int> stack;

        // Push the start vertex onto the stack
        stack.push(startVertex);
        while (!stack.empty()) {
```

```
            // Pop a vertex from the stack
            int currentVertex = stack.top();
            stack.pop();
            // Process the current vertex if not visited
            if (!visited[currentVertex]) {
                std::cout << currentVertex << " ";
                visited[currentVertex] = true;
            }
            // Push adjacent vertices onto the stack
            for (const auto& neighbor : adjacencyList[currentVertex]) {
                if (!visited[neighbor]) {
                    stack.push(neighbor);
                }
            }
        }
    }
};
int main() {
    // Create a graph with 5 vertices
    Graph graph(5);
    // Add edges to the graph
    graph.addEdge(0, 1);
    graph.addEdge(0, 4);
    graph.addEdge(1, 2);
    graph.addEdge(1, 3);
    graph.addEdge(1, 4);
    graph.addEdge(2, 3);
    graph.addEdge(3, 4);
    // Perform DFS starting from vertex 0
    std::cout << "Depth-First Search starting from vertex 0: ";
    graph.DFS(0);
    std::cout << std::endl;
    return 0;
```

```
}
```

In this example, the Graph class has a member variable adjacencyList, which is a vector of lists representing the adjacency list. The addEdge function is used to add an edge to the graph, and the DFS function is used to perform Depth-First Search starting from a specified vertex.

The DFS algorithm uses a stack to keep track of vertices to visit. The visited vector is used to mark whether a vertex has been visited to avoid revisiting the same vertex. The DFS traversal starts from a specified vertex (startVertex in this case) and explores as deep as possible before backtracking.

8.4.BFS

Below is an example of Breadth-First Search (BFS) implemented using a class in C++. In this example, the graph is represented using an adjacency list.

```
#include <iostream>
#include <list>
#include <vector>
#include <queue>
class Graph {
private:
   int numVertices;
   std::vector<std::list<int>> adjacencyList;
public:
   // Constructor
   Graph(int vertices) : numVertices(vertices), adjacencyList(vertices) {}
   // Function to add an edge to the graph
   void addEdge(int source, int destination) {
      if (source >= 0 && source < numVertices && destination >= 0 && destination <
numVertices) {
         adjacencyList[source].push_back(destination);
      } else {
         std::cerr << "Invalid vertices for edge addition." << std::endl;
      }
   }
   // Function to perform Breadth-First Search
   void BFS(int startVertex) {
      // Vector to keep track of visited vertices
      std::vector<bool> visited(numVertices, false);
      // Queue for BFS traversal
      std::queue<int> queue;
      // Enqueue the start vertex
      queue.push(startVertex);
      visited[startVertex] = true;
      while (!queue.empty()) {
```

```
            // Dequeue a vertex from the queue
            int currentVertex = queue.front();
            queue.pop();
            // Process the current vertex
            std::cout << currentVertex << " ";
            // Enqueue adjacent vertices that haven't been visited
            for (const auto& neighbor : adjacencyList[currentVertex]) {
                if (!visited[neighbor]) {
                    queue.push(neighbor);
                    visited[neighbor] = true;
                }
            }
        }
    }
};
int main() {
    // Create a graph with 5 vertices
    Graph graph(5);
    // Add edges to the graph
    graph.addEdge(0, 1);
    graph.addEdge(0, 4);
    graph.addEdge(1, 2);
    graph.addEdge(1, 3);
    graph.addEdge(1, 4);
    graph.addEdge(2, 3);
    graph.addEdge(3, 4);
    // Perform BFS starting from vertex 0
    std::cout << "Breadth-First Search starting from vertex 0: ";
    graph.BFS(0);
    std::cout << std::endl;
    return 0;
}
```

In this example, the Graph class has a member variable adjacencyList, which is a vector of lists representing the adjacency list. The addEdge function is used to add an edge to the graph, and the BFS function is used to perform Breadth-First Search starting from a specified vertex.

The BFS algorithm uses a queue to keep track of vertices to visit. The visited vector is used to mark whether a vertex has been visited to avoid revisiting the same vertex. The BFS traversal starts from a specified vertex (startVertex in this case) and explores all neighbors at the current level before moving to the next level.

8.5. Detect a cycle in a directed graph

Detecting a cycle in a directed graph can be achieved using Depth-First Search (DFS). Below is an example of detecting a cycle in a directed graph using a class in C++:

```
#include <iostream>
#include <vector>
#include <list>
class Graph {
private:
    int numVertices;
    std::vector<std::list<int>> adjacencyList;
public:
    // Constructor
    Graph(int vertices) : numVertices(vertices), adjacencyList(vertices) {}
    // Function to add a directed edge to the graph
    void addEdge(int source, int destination) {
        if (source >= 0 && source < numVertices && destination >= 0 && destination < numVertices) {
            adjacencyList[source].push_back(destination);
        } else {
            std::cerr << "Invalid vertices for edge addition." << std::endl;
        }
    }
    // Function to perform DFS and detect a cycle
    bool isCyclicDFS(int vertex, std::vector<bool>& visited, std::vector<bool>& recursionStack) {
        visited[vertex] = true;
        recursionStack[vertex] = true;
        // Explore all adjacent vertices
        for (const auto& neighbor : adjacencyList[vertex]) {
            if (!visited[neighbor]) {
                if (isCyclicDFS(neighbor, visited, recursionStack)) {
                    return true;
                }
```

```
            } else if (recursionStack[neighbor]) {
                // If the neighbor is already in the recursion stack, a cycle is detected
                return true;
            }
        }
        // Remove the current vertex from the recursion stack
        recursionStack[vertex] = false;
        return false;
    }
    // Function to check if the directed graph has a cycle
    bool hasCycle() {
        // Vector to keep track of visited vertices
        std::vector<bool> visited(numVertices, false);
        // Vector to keep track of vertices in the current recursion stack
        std::vector<bool> recursionStack(numVertices, false);
        // Perform DFS from each vertex
        for (int i = 0; i < numVertices; ++i) {
            if (!visited[i]) {
                if (isCyclicDFS(i, visited, recursionStack)) {
                    return true; // If a cycle is detected from any vertex, return true
                }
            }
        }
        return false; // No cycle detected
    }
};
int main() {
    // Create a directed graph with 4 vertices
    Graph graph(4);
    // Add directed edges to the graph
    graph.addEdge(0, 1);
    graph.addEdge(0, 2);
    graph.addEdge(1, 2);
```

```
    graph.addEdge(2, 0);
    graph.addEdge(2, 3);
    graph.addEdge(3, 3);
    // Check if the directed graph has a cycle
    if (graph.hasCycle()) {
        std::cout << "The directed graph has a cycle." << std::endl;
    } else {
        std::cout << "The directed graph does not have a cycle." << std::endl;
    }
    return 0;
}
```

In this example, the Graph class has a member variable adjacencyList, which is a vector of lists representing the adjacency list for a directed graph. The addEdge function is used to add a directed edge to the graph.

The isCyclicDFS function performs a Depth-First Search (DFS) and checks if there is a cycle starting from a given vertex. The hasCycle function iterates through all vertices and calls isCyclicDFS for each unvisited vertex.

If a cycle is detected during the DFS, the program returns true. Otherwise, it returns false, indicating that the directed graph does not have a cycle.

8.6. Detect a cycle in a undirected graph

Detecting a cycle in an undirected graph can be achieved using Depth-First Search (DFS). Below is an example of detecting a cycle in an undirected graph using a class in C++:

```
#include <iostream>
#include <vector>
#include <list>
class Graph {
private:
   int numVertices;
   std::vector<std::list<int>> adjacencyList;
public:
   // Constructor
   Graph(int vertices) : numVertices(vertices), adjacencyList(vertices) {}
   // Function to add an undirected edge to the graph
   void addEdge(int source, int destination) {
      if (source >= 0 && source < numVertices && destination >= 0 && destination <
numVertices) {
         adjacencyList[source].push_back(destination);
         adjacencyList[destination].push_back(source); // For undirected graph
      } else {
         std::cerr << "Invalid vertices for edge addition." << std::endl;
      }
   }
   // Function to perform DFS and detect a cycle
   bool isCyclicDFS(int vertex, int parent, std::vector<bool>& visited) {
      visited[vertex] = true;
      // Explore all adjacent vertices
      for (const auto& neighbor : adjacencyList[vertex]) {
         if (!visited[neighbor]) {
            if (isCyclicDFS(neighbor, vertex, visited)) {
               return true;
            }
         } else if (neighbor != parent) {
```

```
                // If the neighbor is visited and not the parent, a cycle is detected
                return true;
            }
        }
        return false;
    }
    // Function to check if the undirected graph has a cycle
    bool hasCycle() {
        // Vector to keep track of visited vertices
        std::vector<bool> visited(numVertices, false);

        // Perform DFS from each vertex
        for (int i = 0; i < numVertices; ++i) {
            if (!visited[i]) {
                if (isCyclicDFS(i, -1, visited)) {
                    return true; // If a cycle is detected from any vertex, return true
                }
            }
        }
        return false; // No cycle detected
    }
};
int main() {
    // Create an undirected graph with 4 vertices
    Graph graph(4);
    // Add undirected edges to the graph
    graph.addEdge(0, 1);
    graph.addEdge(1, 2);
    graph.addEdge(2, 0);
    graph.addEdge(1, 3);
    // Check if the undirected graph has a cycle
    if (graph.hasCycle()) {
        std::cout << "The undirected graph has a cycle." << std::endl;
```

```
    } else {
        std::cout << "The undirected graph does not have a cycle." << std::endl;
    }
    return 0;
}
```

In this example, the Graph class has a member variable adjacencyList, which is a vector of lists representing the adjacency list for an undirected graph. The addEdge function is used to add an undirected edge to the graph.

The isCyclicDFS function performs a Depth-First Search (DFS) and checks if there is a cycle starting from a given vertex. The hasCycle function iterates through all vertices and calls isCyclicDFS for each unvisited vertex.

If a cycle is detected during the DFS, the program returns true. Otherwise, it returns false, indicating that the undirected graph does not have a cycle.

8.7. Bellman –ford algorithm for finding the shortest path in a weighted graph

The Bellman-Ford algorithm is used to find the shortest paths from a source vertex to all other vertices in a weighted graph, even if the graph contains negative weight edges (as long as it doesn't contain negative weight cycles). Below is an example of implementing the Bellman-Ford algorithm using a class in C++:

```
#include <iostream>
#include <vector>
#include <climits>
class Graph {
private:
  int numVertices;
  std::vector<std::vector<std::pair<int, int>>> adjacencyList;
public:
  // Constructor
  Graph(int vertices) : numVertices(vertices), adjacencyList(vertices) {}
  // Function to add a weighted directed edge to the graph
  void addEdge(int source, int destination, int weight) {
    if (source >= 0 && source < numVertices && destination >= 0 && destination <
numVertices) {
      adjacencyList[source].push_back({destination, weight});
    } else {
      std::cerr << "Invalid vertices for edge addition." << std::endl;
    }
  }
  // Function to perform Bellman-Ford algorithm
  std::vector<int> bellmanFord(int source) {
    std::vector<int> distance(numVertices, INT_MAX);
    // Initialize distance to the source as 0
    distance[source] = 0;
    // Relax edges repeatedly (V-1) times
    for (int i = 0; i < numVertices - 1; ++i) {
      for (int u = 0; u < numVertices; ++u) {
        for (const auto& neighbor : adjacencyList[u]) {
```

```
                int v = neighbor.first;
                int weight = neighbor.second;
                // Relax the edge (u, v)
                if (distance[u] != INT_MAX && distance[u] + weight < distance[v]) {
                    distance[v] = distance[u] + weight;
                }
            }
        }
    }
    // Check for negative weight cycles
    for (int u = 0; u < numVertices; ++u) {
        for (const auto& neighbor : adjacencyList[u]) {
            int v = neighbor.first;
            int weight = neighbor.second;
            // If relaxation is still possible, there is a negative weight cycle
            if (distance[u] != INT_MAX && distance[u] + weight < distance[v]) {
                std::cerr << "Graph contains a negative weight cycle." << std::endl;
                return std::vector<int>();
            }
        }
    }
    return distance;
  }
};
int main() {
    // Create a weighted directed graph with 5 vertices
    Graph graph(5);
    // Add weighted directed edges to the graph
    graph.addEdge(0, 1, -1);
    graph.addEdge(0, 2, 4);
    graph.addEdge(1, 2, 3);
    graph.addEdge(1, 3, 2);
    graph.addEdge(1, 4, 2);
```

```
    graph.addEdge(3, 2, 5);
    graph.addEdge(3, 1, 1);
    graph.addEdge(4, 3, -3);
    // Perform Bellman-Ford algorithm starting from vertex 0
    int sourceVertex = 0;
    std::vector<int> distances = graph.bellmanFord(sourceVertex);
    // Display the shortest distances from the source vertex
    if (!distances.empty()) {
        std::cout << "Shortest distances from vertex " << sourceVertex << " to all other
vertices:" << std::endl;
        for (int i = 0; i < graph.getNumVertices(); ++i) {
            std::cout << "Vertex " << i << ": " << distances[i] << std::endl;
        }
    }
    return 0;
}
```

In this example, the Graph class has a member variable adjacencyList, which is a vector of vectors of pairs representing the adjacency list for a weighted directed graph. The addEdge function is used to add a weighted directed edge to the graph. The bellmanFord function performs the Bellman-Ford algorithm, and it returns a vector containing the shortest distances from the source vertex to all other vertices. If there is a negative weight cycle, the function returns an empty vector. This example creates a graph with 5 vertices and performs the Bellman-Ford algorithm starting from vertex 0, displaying the shortest distances from vertex 0 to all other vertices.

8.8 Dijkstra's Algorithm

Dijkstra's algorithm is used to find the shortest paths from a source vertex to all other vertices in a weighted graph with non-negative edge weights. Below is an example of implementing Dijkstra's algorithm using a class in C++:

```
#include <iostream>
#include <vector>
#include <queue>
#include <limits>
class Graph {
private:
    int numVertices;
    std::vector<std::vector<std::pair<int, int>>> adjacencyList;
public:
    // Constructor
    Graph(int vertices) : numVertices(vertices), adjacencyList(vertices) {}
    // Function to add a weighted directed edge to the graph
    void addEdge(int source, int destination, int weight) {
        if (source >= 0 && source < numVertices && destination >= 0 && destination <
numVertices) {
            adjacencyList[source].push_back({destination, weight});
        } else {
            std::cerr << "Invalid vertices for edge addition." << std::endl;
        }
    }
    // Function to perform Dijkstra's algorithm
    std::vector<int> dijkstra(int source) {
        std::vector<int> distance(numVertices, std::numeric_limits<int>::max());
        distance[source] = 0;
        // Priority queue to keep track of vertices with their current distances
        std::priority_queue<std::pair<int, int>, std::vector<std::pair<int, int>>,
std::greater<std::pair<int, int>>> pq;
        pq.push({0, source});
        while (!pq.empty()) {
```

```
            int currentVertex = pq.top().second;
            int currentDistance = pq.top().first;
            pq.pop();
            // If the current distance is greater than the stored distance, skip
            if (currentDistance > distance[currentVertex]) {
                continue;
            }
            // Relaxation step
            for (const auto& neighbor : adjacencyList[currentVertex]) {
                int v = neighbor.first;
                int weight = neighbor.second;
                if (distance[currentVertex] + weight < distance[v]) {
                    distance[v] = distance[currentVertex] + weight;
                    pq.push({distance[v], v});
                }
            }
        }
        return distance;
    }
};
int main() {
    // Create a weighted directed graph with 5 vertices
    Graph graph(5);
    // Add weighted directed edges to the graph
    graph.addEdge(0, 1, 4);
    graph.addEdge(0, 2, 2);
    graph.addEdge(1, 2, 5);
    graph.addEdge(1, 3, 10);
    graph.addEdge(2, 3, 3);
    graph.addEdge(3, 4, 7);
    graph.addEdge(4, 0, 1);
    // Perform Dijkstra's algorithm starting from vertex 0
    int sourceVertex = 0;
```

```
    std::vector<int> distances = graph.dijkstra(sourceVertex);
    // Display the shortest distances from the source vertex
    std::cout << "Shortest distances from vertex " << sourceVertex << " to all other vertices:"
<< std::endl;
    for (int i = 0; i < graph.getNumVertices(); ++i) {
        std::cout << "Vertex " << i << ": " << distances[i] << std::endl;
    }
    return 0;
}
```

In this example, the Graph class has a member variable adjacencyList, which is a vector of vectors of pairs representing the adjacency list for a weighted directed graph. The addEdge function is used to add a weighted directed edge to the graph.

The dijkstra function performs Dijkstra's algorithm, and it returns a vector containing the shortest distances from the source vertex to all other vertices.

This example creates a graph with 5 vertices and performs Dijkstra's algorithm starting from vertex 0, displaying the shortest distances from vertex 0 to all other vertices.

8.9. Prim's Algorithm

Prim's algorithm is used to find the minimum spanning tree of a connected, undirected graph. Below is an example of implementing Prim's algorithm using a class in C++:

```
#include <iostream>
#include <vector>
#include <queue>
#include <climits>
class Graph {
private:
  int numVertices;
  std::vector<std::vector<std::pair<int, int>>> adjacencyList;
public:
  // Constructor
  Graph(int vertices) : numVertices(vertices), adjacencyList(vertices) {}
  // Function to add an undirected edge with weight to the graph
  void addEdge(int source, int destination, int weight) {
    if (source >= 0 && source < numVertices && destination >= 0 && destination <
numVertices) {
      adjacencyList[source].push_back({destination, weight});
      adjacencyList[destination].push_back({source, weight});
    } else {
      std::cerr << "Invalid vertices for edge addition." << std::endl;
    }
  }
  // Function to perform Prim's algorithm
  int primMST() {
    // Priority queue to store edges with their weights
    std::priority_queue<std::pair<int, int>, std::vector<std::pair<int, int>>,
std::greater<std::pair<int, int>>> pq;
    // Start with the first vertex
    int startVertex = 0;
    // Vector to keep track of visited vertices
    std::vector<bool> visited(numVertices, false);
```

```
        // Mark the first vertex as visited
        visited[startVertex] = true;
        // Add all edges from the first vertex to the priority queue
        for (const auto& neighbor : adjacencyList[startVertex]) {
            pq.push({neighbor.second, neighbor.first});
        }
        int minCost = 0; // Minimum cost of the minimum spanning tree
        while (!pq.empty()) {
            // Get the edge with the minimum weight
            int weight = pq.top().first;
            int currentVertex = pq.top().second;
            pq.pop();
            // If the current vertex is already visited, skip
            if (visited[currentVertex]) {
                continue;
            }
            // Mark the current vertex as visited
            visited[currentVertex] = true;
            // Add the weight to the minimum cost
            minCost += weight;
            // Add all edges from the current vertex to the priority queue
            for (const auto& neighbor : adjacencyList[currentVertex]) {
                pq.push({neighbor.second, neighbor.first});
            }
        }
        return minCost;
    }
};
int main() {
    // Create an undirected graph with 5 vertices
    Graph graph(5);
    // Add undirected edges with weights to the graph
    graph.addEdge(0, 1, 2);
```

```
    graph.addEdge(0, 3, 1);
    graph.addEdge(1, 2, 4);
    graph.addEdge(1, 3, 3);
    graph.addEdge(1, 4, 5);
    graph.addEdge(2, 4, 1);
    graph.addEdge(3, 4, 6);
    // Perform Prim's algorithm and get the minimum cost of the minimum spanning tree
    int minCost = graph.primMST();
    // Display the minimum cost
    std::cout << "Minimum cost of the minimum spanning tree: " << minCost << std::endl;
    return 0;
}
```

In this example, the Graph class has a member variable adjacencyList, which is a vector of vectors of pairs representing the adjacency list for an undirected graph. The addEdge function is used to add an undirected edge with weight to the graph.

The primMST function performs Prim's algorithm and returns the minimum cost of the minimum spanning tree. The algorithm starts from an arbitrary vertex and greedily adds the minimum-weight edges that connect the current tree to the unvisited vertices.

This example creates a graph with 5 vertices, adds undirected edges with weights, performs Prim's algorithm, and displays the minimum cost of the minimum spanning tree.

8.10.Kruskal's algorithm for finding the minimum spanning tree

Kruskal's algorithm is a greedy algorithm used to find the minimum spanning tree in a connected, undirected graph. Below is an example of implementing Kruskal's algorithm using a class in C++:

```
#include <iostream>
#include <vector>
#include <algorithm>
class Graph {
private:
    int numVertices;
    std::vector<std::pair<int, std::pair<int, int>>> edges;
public:
    // Constructor
    Graph(int vertices) : numVertices(vertices) {}
    // Function to add an undirected edge with weight to the graph
    void addEdge(int source, int destination, int weight) {
        if (source >= 0 && source < numVertices && destination >= 0 && destination <
numVertices) {
            edges.push_back({weight, {source, destination}});
        } else {
            std::cerr << "Invalid vertices for edge addition." << std::endl;
        }
    }
    // Function to perform Kruskal's algorithm
    int kruskalMST() {
        // Sort edges in ascending order based on weights
        std::sort(edges.begin(), edges.end());

        // Vector to keep track of parent for each vertex (used for detecting cycles)
        std::vector<int> parent(numVertices);

        // Initialize parent for each vertex to itself
        for (int i = 0; i < numVertices; ++i) {
```

```
            parent[i] = i;
        }
        int minCost = 0; // Minimum cost of the minimum spanning tree
        int edgesIncluded = 0; // Number of edges included in the minimum spanning tree
        // Iterate through sorted edges
        for (const auto& edge : edges) {
            int weight = edge.first;
            int source = edge.second.first;
            int destination = edge.second.second;
            // Find the parent of the source and destination vertices
            int rootSource = findParent(parent, source);
            int rootDestination = findParent(parent, destination);
            // If adding the current edge doesn't form a cycle, include it in the minimum spanning
tree
            if (rootSource != rootDestination) {
                minCost += weight;
                unionSets(parent, rootSource, rootDestination);
                edgesIncluded++;
                // If all vertices are included, break out of the loop
                if (edgesIncluded == numVertices - 1) {
                    break;
                }
            }
        }
        return minCost;
    }
private:
    // Function to find the parent of a vertex using path compression
    int findParent(std::vector<int>& parent, int vertex) {
        if (parent[vertex] != vertex) {
            parent[vertex] = findParent(parent, parent[vertex]);
        }
        return parent[vertex];
```

```
    }
    // Function to union two sets using rank
    void unionSets(std::vector<int>& parent, int root1, int root2) {
        if (root1 != root2) {
            parent[root2] = root1;
        }
    }
};
int main() {
    // Create an undirected graph with 5 vertices
    Graph graph(5);
    // Add undirected edges with weights to the graph
    graph.addEdge(0, 1, 2);
    graph.addEdge(0, 3, 1);
    graph.addEdge(1, 2, 4);
    graph.addEdge(1, 3, 3);
    graph.addEdge(1, 4, 5);
    graph.addEdge(2, 4, 1);
    graph.addEdge(3, 4, 6);
    // Perform Kruskal's algorithm and get the minimum cost of the minimum spanning tree
    int minCost = graph.kruskalMST();
    // Display the minimum cost
    std::cout << "Minimum cost of the minimum spanning tree: " << minCost << std::endl;
    return 0;
}
```

In this example, the Graph class has a member variable edges, which is a vector of pairs representing the edges of the graph with their weights. The addEdge function is used to add an undirected edge with weight to the graph.

The kruskalMST function performs Kruskal's algorithm. It sorts the edges in ascending order based on weights and iterates through the sorted edges, including each edge in the minimum spanning tree if adding it doesn't form a cycle. The findParent and unionSets functions are used for efficient union-find operations with path compression and rank. The algorithm continues until the number of edges included in the minimum spanning tree is equal to the number of vertices minus 1.

This example creates a graph with 5 vertices, adds undirected edges with weights, performs Kruskal's algorithm, and displays the minimum cost of the minimum spanning tree.

9.HASHING

9.1. Implement a hash table

Here's an example of implementing a basic hash table using a class in C++:

```
#include <iostream>
#include <vector>
#include <list>
#include <iterator>
// HashTable class template
template <typename KeyType, typename ValueType>
class HashTable {
private:
   // Bucket type (using linked list to handle collisions)
   using Bucket = std::list<std::pair<KeyType, ValueType>>;
   // Vector of buckets
   std::vector<Bucket> table;
   // Hash function to determine the bucket index
   std::size_t hashFunction(const KeyType& key) const {
      // Example: simple hash function using the length of the key
      return std::hash<KeyType>{}(key) % table.size();
   }
public:
   // Constructor with the initial number of buckets
   HashTable(std::size_t initialSize = 10) : table(initialSize) {}
   // Function to insert a key-value pair into the hash table
   void insert(const KeyType& key, const ValueType& value) {
      std::size_t index = hashFunction(key);
      table[index].emplace_back(key, value);
   }
   // Function to retrieve the value associated with a key
   // Returns true if key is found, false otherwise
   bool find(const KeyType& key, ValueType& value) const {
      std::size_t index = hashFunction(key);
      for (const auto& entry : table[index]) {
```

```
            if (entry.first == key) {
                value = entry.second;
                return true; // Key found
            }
        }
        return false; // Key not found
    }
    // Function to remove a key-value pair from the hash table
    // Returns true if key is found and removed, false otherwise
    bool remove(const KeyType& key) {
        std::size_t index = hashFunction(key);
        auto& bucket = table[index];
        for (auto it = bucket.begin(); it != bucket.end(); ++it) {
            if (it->first == key) {
                bucket.erase(it);
                return true; // Key found and removed
            }
        }
        return false; // Key not found
    }
    // Function to display the contents of the hash table
    void display() const {
        for (std::size_t i = 0; i < table.size(); ++i) {
            std::cout << "Bucket " << i << ": ";
            for (const auto& entry : table[i]) {
                std::cout << "(" << entry.first << ", " << entry.second << ") ";
            }
            std::cout << std::endl;
        }
    }
};
int main() {
    // Create a hash table with an initial size of 5 buckets
```

```
    HashTable<std::string, int> myHashTable(5);
    // Insert key-value pairs
    myHashTable.insert("Alice", 25);
    myHashTable.insert("Bob", 30);
    myHashTable.insert("Charlie", 22);
    // Display the contents of the hash table
    std::cout << "Initial Hash Table:" << std::endl;
    myHashTable.display();
    // Find and display values associated with keys
    int value;
    if (myHashTable.find("Bob", value)) {
        std::cout << "Value associated with key 'Bob': " << value << std::endl;
    } else {
        std::cout << "Key 'Bob' not found." << std::endl;
    }
    // Remove a key-value pair
    if (myHashTable.remove("Alice")) {
        std::cout << "Key 'Alice' removed." << std::endl;
    } else {
        std::cout << "Key 'Alice' not found." << std::endl;
    }
    // Display the updated contents of the hash table
    std::cout << "\nUpdated Hash Table:" << std::endl;
    myHashTable.display();
    return 0;
}
```

In this example, the HashTable class template has a vector of buckets, and each bucket is implemented as a linked list to handle collisions. The hashFunction method determines the index of the bucket for a given key using a basic hash function.

The insert, find, and remove methods are provided to add key-value pairs, search for values based on keys, and remove key-value pairs, respectively. The display method is used to print the contents of the hash table for demonstration purposes.

This is a basic implementation, and in real-world scenarios, more advanced techniques such as dynamic resizing, load factor management, and collision resolution strategies might be employed for a more robust hash table.

9.2.Resolve collisions using open addressing

Open addressing is a technique to resolve collisions in a hash table by searching for the next available slot in the table when a collision occurs. Here's an example of implementing a hash table with open addressing using a class in C++:

```
#include <iostream>
#include <vector>
#include <functional>
template <typename KeyType, typename ValueType>
class HashTable {
private:
   // Bucket type with key-value pair
   struct Bucket {
      KeyType key;
      ValueType value;
      bool occupied; // Flag to track if the bucket is occupied
   };
   // Vector of buckets
   std::vector<Bucket> table;
   // Hash function to determine the bucket index
   std::size_t hashFunction(const KeyType& key) const {
      return std::hash<KeyType>{}(key) % table.size();
   }
   // Function to find the next available slot using linear probing
   std::size_t linearProbe(std::size_t index) const {
      std::size_t originalIndex = index;
      do {
         index = (index + 1) % table.size();
      } while (table[index].occupied && index != originalIndex);
      return index;
   }
public:
   // Constructor with the initial number of buckets
```

```
    HashTable(std::size_t initialSize = 10) : table(initialSize, Bucket{KeyType{},
ValueType{}, false}) {}
    // Function to insert a key-value pair into the hash table
    void insert(const KeyType& key, const ValueType& value) {
        std::size_t index = hashFunction(key);
        // If the bucket is occupied, find the next available slot
        if (table[index].occupied) {
            index = linearProbe(index);
        }
        // Insert the key-value pair into the bucket
        table[index].key = key;
        table[index].value = value;
        table[index].occupied = true;
    }
    // Function to retrieve the value associated with a key
    // Returns true if key is found, false otherwise
    bool find(const KeyType& key, ValueType& value) const {
        std::size_t index = hashFunction(key);
        std::size_t originalIndex = index;
        // Search for the key using linear probing
        do {
            if (table[index].occupied && table[index].key == key) {
                value = table[index].value;
                return true; // Key found
            }
            index = (index + 1) % table.size();
        } while (index != originalIndex && table[index].occupied);
        return false; // Key not found
    }
    // Function to remove a key-value pair from the hash table
    // Returns true if key is found and removed, false otherwise
    bool remove(const KeyType& key) {
        std::size_t index = hashFunction(key);
```

```
        std::size_t originalIndex = index;
        // Search for the key using linear probing
        do {
            if (table[index].occupied && table[index].key == key) {
                table[index].occupied = false;
                return true; // Key found and removed
            }
            index = (index + 1) % table.size();
        } while (index != originalIndex && table[index].occupied);
        return false; // Key not found
    }
    // Function to display the contents of the hash table
    void display() const {
        for (std::size_t i = 0; i < table.size(); ++i) {
            if (table[i].occupied) {
                std::cout << "Bucket " << i << ": (" << table[i].key << ", " << table[i].value << ")"
<< std::endl;
            } else {
                std::cout << "Bucket " << i << ": Empty" << std::endl;
            }
        }
    }
};
int main() {
    // Create a hash table with an initial size of 5 buckets
    HashTable<std::string, int> myHashTable(5);
    // Insert key-value pairs
    myHashTable.insert("Alice", 25);
    myHashTable.insert("Bob", 30);
    myHashTable.insert("Charlie", 22);
    // Display the contents of the hash table
    std::cout << "Initial Hash Table:" << std::endl;
    myHashTable.display();
```

```
    // Find and display values associated with keys
    int value;
    if (myHashTable.find("Bob", value)) {
        std::cout << "Value associated with key 'Bob': " << value << std::endl;
    } else {
        std::cout << "Key 'Bob' not found." << std::endl;
    }
    // Remove a key-value pair
    if (myHashTable.remove("Alice")) {
        std::cout << "Key 'Alice' removed." << std::endl;
    } else {
        std::cout << "Key 'Alice' not found." << std::endl;
    }
    // Display the updated contents of the hash table
    std::cout << "\nUpdated Hash Table:" << std::endl;
    myHashTable.display();
    return 0;
}
```

In this example, the HashTable class uses linear probing as an open addressing strategy. The linearProbe function is used to find the next available slot by linearly searching for an unoccupied bucket.

The insert, find, and remove methods handle the basic operations, and the display method is used to print the contents of the hash table for demonstration purposes.

Please note that this is a basic implementation, and in practice, other open addressing strategies such as quadratic probing or double hashing might be used for better performance. Additionally, handling edge cases and resizing the table dynamically are important considerations for a fully functional hash table implementation.

9.3. Implement basic hash functions

Below is an example of a basic hash table implementation in C++ using a class with some commonly used hash functions. This example uses separate chaining to handle collisions, where each bucket in the hash table contains a linked list of key-value pairs.

```
#include <iostream>
#include <vector>
#include <list>
#include <functional>
template <typename KeyType, typename ValueType>
class HashTable {
private:
   // Bucket type with key-value pair
   struct Bucket {
      KeyType key;
      ValueType value;
   };
   // Vector of buckets (linked lists for separate chaining)
   std::vector<std::list<Bucket>> table;
   // Hash function to determine the bucket index
   std::size_t hashFunction1(const KeyType& key) const {
      // Example 1: std::hash (default hash function in C++)
      return std::hash<KeyType>{}(key) % table.size();
   }
   std::size_t hashFunction2(const KeyType& key) const {
      // Example 2: Simple sum of ASCII values of characters in the key
      std::size_t hashValue = 0;
      for (const auto& ch : key) {
         hashValue += static_cast<std::size_t>(ch);
      }
      return hashValue % table.size();
   }
   std::size_t hashFunction3(const KeyType& key) const {
      // Example 3: Custom hash function using bitwise XOR
```

```
        std::size_t hashValue = 0;
        for (const auto& ch : key) {
            hashValue ^= static_cast<std::size_t>(ch);
        }
        return hashValue % table.size();
    }
public:
    // Constructor with the initial number of buckets
    HashTable(std::size_t initialSize = 10) : table(initialSize) {}
    // Function to insert a key-value pair into the hash table
    void insert(const KeyType& key, const ValueType& value) {
        std::size_t index = hashFunction1(key);  // Change the hash function if needed
        // Insert the key-value pair into the bucket
        table[index].push_back({key, value});
    }
    // Function to retrieve the value associated with a key
    // Returns true if key is found, false otherwise
    bool find(const KeyType& key, ValueType& value) const {
        std::size_t index = hashFunction1(key);  // Change the hash function if needed
        // Search for the key in the bucket
        for (const auto& entry : table[index]) {
            if (entry.key == key) {
                value = entry.value;
                return true; // Key found
            }
        }
        return false; // Key not found
    }
    // Function to remove a key-value pair from the hash table
    // Returns true if key is found and removed, false otherwise
    bool remove(const KeyType& key) {
        std::size_t index = hashFunction1(key);  // Change the hash function if needed
        auto& bucket = table[index];
```

```
        // Search for the key in the bucket and remove it
        auto it = std::find_if(bucket.begin(), bucket.end(), [&](const auto& entry) {
            return entry.key == key;
        });
        if (it != bucket.end()) {
            bucket.erase(it);
            return true; // Key found and removed
        }
        return false; // Key not found
    }
    // Function to display the contents of the hash table
    void display() const {
        for (std::size_t i = 0; i < table.size(); ++i) {
            std::cout << "Bucket " << i << ": ";
            for (const auto& entry : table[i]) {
                std::cout << "(" << entry.key << ", " << entry.value << ") ";
            }
            std::cout << std::endl;
        }
    }
};
int main() {
    // Create a hash table with an initial size of 5 buckets
    HashTable<std::string, int> myHashTable(5);
    // Insert key-value pairs
    myHashTable.insert("Alice", 25);
    myHashTable.insert("Bob", 30);
    myHashTable.insert("Charlie", 22);
    // Display the contents of the hash table
    std::cout << "Initial Hash Table:" << std::endl;
    myHashTable.display();
    // Find and display values associated with keys
    int value;
```

```
    if (myHashTable.find("Bob", value)) {
        std::cout << "Value associated with key 'Bob': " << value << std::endl;
    } else {
        std::cout << "Key 'Bob' not found." << std::endl;
    }
    // Remove a key-value pair
    if (myHashTable.remove("Alice")) {
        std::cout << "Key 'Alice' removed." << std::endl;
    } else {
        std::cout << "Key 'Alice' not found." << std::endl;
    }
    // Display the updated contents of the hash table
    std::cout << "\nUpdated Hash Table:" << std::endl;
    myHashTable.display();
    return 0;
}
```

In this example, three different hash functions (hashFunction1, hashFunction2, and hashFunction3) are provided as examples. You can choose the hash function that suits your requirements or define your own custom hash function.

Remember that choosing a good hash function is crucial for the performance of the hash table, and the hash function may vary based on the data being stored. The hash functions provided in this example are simple and may not be suitable for all scenarios. For real-world applications, you may need to design or choose hash functions that distribute keys more evenly across the hash table to minimize collisions.

9.4. Perform insert, delete and search operations in a hash table

Below is an example of a HashTable class in C++ that supports insert, delete, and search operations. The hash table uses separate chaining to handle collisions, where each bucket in the hash table contains a linked list of key-value pairs.

```
#include <iostream>
#include <vector>
#include <list>
#include <functional>
#include <iterator>
template <typename KeyType, typename ValueType>
class HashTable {
private:
   // Bucket type with key-value pair
   struct Bucket {
      KeyType key;
      ValueType value;
   };
   // Vector of buckets (linked lists for separate chaining)
   std::vector<std::list<Bucket>> table;
   // Hash function to determine the bucket index
   std::size_t hashFunction(const KeyType& key) const {
      // Example: Using std::hash as the hash function
      return std::hash<KeyType>{}(key) % table.size();
   }
public:
   // Constructor with the initial number of buckets
   HashTable(std::size_t initialSize = 10) : table(initialSize) {}
   // Function to insert a key-value pair into the hash table
   void insert(const KeyType& key, const ValueType& value) {
      std::size_t index = hashFunction(key);
      auto& bucket = table[index];
      // Check if the key already exists in the bucket
      auto it = std::find_if(bucket.begin(), bucket.end(), [&](const auto& entry) {
```

```
            return entry.key == key;
        });
        // If key exists, update the value; otherwise, insert a new key-value pair
        if (it != bucket.end()) {
            it->value = value;
        } else {
            bucket.push_back({key, value});
        }
    }
    // Function to retrieve the value associated with a key
    // Returns true if key is found, false otherwise
    bool find(const KeyType& key, ValueType& value) const {
        std::size_t index = hashFunction(key);
        const auto& bucket = table[index];
        // Search for the key in the bucket
        auto it = std::find_if(bucket.begin(), bucket.end(), [&](const auto& entry) {
            return entry.key == key;
        });
        // If key is found, update the value parameter and return true
        if (it != bucket.end()) {
            value = it->value;
            return true;
        }
        return false; // Key not found
    }
    // Function to remove a key-value pair from the hash table
    // Returns true if key is found and removed, false otherwise
    bool remove(const KeyType& key) {
        std::size_t index = hashFunction(key);
        auto& bucket = table[index];
        // Search for the key in the bucket and remove it
        auto it = std::find_if(bucket.begin(), bucket.end(), [&](const auto& entry) {
            return entry.key == key;
```

```
        });
        // If key is found, remove it and return true
        if (it != bucket.end()) {
            bucket.erase(it);
            return true;
        }
        return false; // Key not found
    }
    // Function to display the contents of the hash table
    void display() const {
        for (std::size_t i = 0; i < table.size(); ++i) {
            std::cout << "Bucket " << i << ": ";
            for (const auto& entry : table[i]) {
                std::cout << "(" << entry.key << ", " << entry.value << ") ";
            }
            std::cout << std::endl;
        }
    }
};
int main() {
    // Create a hash table with an initial size of 5 buckets
    HashTable<std::string, int> myHashTable(5);
    // Insert key-value pairs
    myHashTable.insert("Alice", 25);
    myHashTable.insert("Bob", 30);
    myHashTable.insert("Charlie", 22);
    // Display the contents of the hash table
    std::cout << "Initial Hash Table:" << std::endl;
    myHashTable.display();
    // Find and display values associated with keys
    int value;
    if (myHashTable.find("Bob", value)) {
        std::cout << "Value associated with key 'Bob': " << value << std::endl;
```

```
    } else {
        std::cout << "Key 'Bob' not found." << std::endl;
    }
    // Remove a key-value pair
    if (myHashTable.remove("Alice")) {
        std::cout << "Key 'Alice' removed." << std::endl;
    } else {
        std::cout << "Key 'Alice' not found." << std::endl;
    }
    // Display the updated contents of the hash table
    std::cout << "\nUpdated Hash Table:" << std::endl;
    myHashTable.display();
    return 0;
}
```

In this example, the HashTable class provides insert, find, remove, and display methods. The insert method updates the value if the key already exists in the hash table; otherwise, it inserts a new key-value pair. The find method searches for a key and returns the associated value if found. The remove method removes a key-value pair from the hash table.

The display method is included to print the contents of the hash table for demonstration purposes. You can customize the hash function according to your specific requirements.

10.HEAP

10.1. Implement a binary heap (Min and Max heap)

Below is an example of implementing a binary heap (both MinHeap and MaxHeap) using a class in C++. A binary heap is a complete binary tree where the value of each node is either greater than or equal to (MaxHeap) or less than or equal to (MinHeap) the values of its children.

```
#include <iostream>
#include <vector>
// BinaryHeap class template
template <typename T>
class BinaryHeap {
private:
    std::vector<T> heap;
    bool isMinHeap; // Flag to indicate MinHeap or MaxHeap
public:
    // Constructor
    BinaryHeap(bool isMin = true) : isMinHeap(isMin) {}
    // Function to insert a value into the heap
    void insert(T value) {
        heap.push_back(value);
        heapifyUp(heap.size() - 1);
    }
    // Function to extract the root value (Min or Max value)
    T extractRoot() {
        if (heap.empty()) {
            throw std::out_of_range("Heap is empty");
        }
        T rootValue = heap[0];
        heap[0] = heap.back();
        heap.pop_back();
        heapifyDown(0);
        return rootValue;
    }
```

```
    // Function to get the size of the heap
    std::size_t size() const {
        return heap.size();
    }
    // Function to check if the heap is empty
    bool isEmpty() const {
        return heap.empty();
    }
private:
    // Function to heapify up (move a node up to maintain heap property)
    void heapifyUp(std::size_t index) {
        while (index > 0) {
            std::size_t parent = (index - 1) / 2;
            // For MinHeap, swap if the current node is smaller than its parent
            // For MaxHeap, swap if the current node is greater than its parent
            if ((isMinHeap && heap[index] < heap[parent]) ||
                (!isMinHeap && heap[index] > heap[parent])) {
                std::swap(heap[index], heap[parent]);
                index = parent;
            } else {
                break;
            }
        }
    }
    // Function to heapify down (move a node down to maintain heap property)
    void heapifyDown(std::size_t index) {
        std::size_t leftChild, rightChild, targetChild;
        while (true) {
            leftChild = 2 * index + 1;
            rightChild = 2 * index + 2;
            targetChild = index;
            // For MinHeap, find the smallest child
            // For MaxHeap, find the largest child
```

```
            if (leftChild < heap.size() &&
                ((isMinHeap && heap[leftChild] < heap[targetChild]) ||
                 (!isMinHeap && heap[leftChild] > heap[targetChild]))) {
                targetChild = leftChild;
            }
            if (rightChild < heap.size() &&
                ((isMinHeap && heap[rightChild] < heap[targetChild]) ||
                 (!isMinHeap && heap[rightChild] > heap[targetChild]))) {
                targetChild = rightChild;
            }
            if (targetChild != index) {
                std::swap(heap[index], heap[targetChild]);
                index = targetChild;
            } else {
                break;
            }
        }
    }
};
int main() {
    // Example of MinHeap
    BinaryHeap<int> minHeap(true);
    minHeap.insert(4);
    minHeap.insert(2);
    minHeap.insert(7);
    minHeap.insert(5);
    minHeap.insert(1);
    std::cout << "MinHeap Size: " << minHeap.size() << std::endl;
    while (!minHeap.isEmpty()) {
        std::cout << "MinHeap Root: " << minHeap.extractRoot() << std::endl;
    }
    // Example of MaxHeap
    BinaryHeap<int> maxHeap(false);
```

```
    maxHeap.insert(4);
    maxHeap.insert(2);
    maxHeap.insert(7);
    maxHeap.insert(5);
    maxHeap.insert(1);
    std::cout << "\nMaxHeap Size: " << maxHeap.size() << std::endl;
    while (!maxHeap.isEmpty()) {
        std::cout << "MaxHeap Root: " << maxHeap.extractRoot() << std::endl;
    }
    return 0;
}
```

In this example, the BinaryHeap class template has a vector heap to store the heap elements and a boolean flag isMinHeap to determine whether it is a MinHeap or MaxHeap.

The insert function adds a new element to the heap and maintains the heap property by calling heapifyUp.

The extractRoot function removes and returns the root element (Min or Max value) from the heap and maintains the heap property by calling heapifyDown.

The heapifyUp and heapifyDown functions are responsible for moving nodes up or down, respectively, to maintain the heap property.

The main function demonstrates creating both a MinHeap and a MaxHeap, inserting elements, and extracting the root elements.

10.2. Heap sort

Heap Sort is a comparison-based sorting algorithm that uses a binary heap data structure to build a max-heap (for ascending order) or min-heap (for descending order). Below is an example of implementing Heap Sort using a class in C++:

```
#include <iostream>
#include <vector>
template <typename T>
class HeapSort {
public:
   // Function to perform heap sort on an array
   static void sort(std::vector<T>& arr) {
      int n = arr.size();
      // Build max heap (convert the array to a max heap)
      buildMaxHeap(arr, n);
      // Extract elements from the max heap one by one
      for (int i = n - 1; i > 0; --i) {
         // Move the current root (maximum) element to the end
         std::swap(arr[0], arr[i]);
         // Call heapify on the reduced heap
         heapify(arr, i, 0);
      }
   }
private:
   // Function to build a max heap from the array
   static void buildMaxHeap(std::vector<T>& arr, int n) {
      // Start from the last non-leaf node and heapify all nodes
      for (int i = n / 2 - 1; i >= 0; --i) {
         heapify(arr, n, i);
      }
   }
   // Function to heapify a subtree rooted with the given index
   static void heapify(std::vector<T>& arr, int n, int index) {
      int largest = index; // Initialize the largest as root
```

```
        int left = 2 * index + 1; // Left child index
        int right = 2 * index + 2; // Right child index
        // If the left child is larger than the root
        if (left < n && arr[left] > arr[largest]) {
            largest = left;
        }
        // If the right child is larger than the largest so far
        if (right < n && arr[right] > arr[largest]) {
            largest = right;
        }
        // If the largest is not the root, swap and heapify the affected sub-tree
        if (largest != index) {
            std::swap(arr[index], arr[largest]);
            heapify(arr, n, largest);
        }
    }
};
int main() {
    // Example usage of HeapSort
    std::vector<int> arr = {12, 11, 13, 5, 6, 7};
    std::cout << "Original Array: ";
    for (int num : arr) {
        std::cout << num << " ";
    }
    std::cout << std::endl;
    // Perform heap sort
    HeapSort<int>::sort(arr);

    std::cout << "Sorted Array: ";
    for (int num : arr) {
        std::cout << num << " ";
    }
    std::cout << std::endl;
```

```
    return 0;
}
```

In this example, the HeapSort class template provides a sort method that takes a vector and sorts it using the Heap Sort algorithm. The buildMaxHeap function builds a max heap from the array, and the heapify function is used to maintain the heap property.

The main function demonstrates the usage of the HeapSort class to sort an array of integers.

Remember that Heap Sort has a time complexity of O(n log n) for the worst, average, and best cases and a space complexity of O(1) since it is an in-place sorting algorithm.

11.PRIORITY QUEUE

11.1. Implement a priority queue using a heap data structure

Below is an example of implementing a priority queue using a max-heap data structure using a class in C++. In this example, the PriorityQueue class is implemented with basic operations such as enqueue (insert), dequeue (extract max), and isEmpty.

```
#include <iostream>
#include <vector>
template <typename T>
class PriorityQueue {
private:
  std::vector<T> maxHeap;
  // Helper function to maintain the max heap property
  void heapifyUp(std::size_t index) {
    while (index > 0) {
      std::size_t parent = (index - 1) / 2;
      if (maxHeap[index] > maxHeap[parent]) {
        std::swap(maxHeap[index], maxHeap[parent]);
        index = parent;
      } else {
        break;
      }
    }
  }
  // Helper function to maintain the max heap property
  void heapifyDown(std::size_t index) {
    std::size_t leftChild, rightChild, targetChild;
    while (true) {
      leftChild = 2 * index + 1;
      rightChild = 2 * index + 2;
      targetChild = index;
      if (leftChild < maxHeap.size() && maxHeap[leftChild] > maxHeap[targetChild]) {
        targetChild = leftChild;
      }
```

```
        if (rightChild < maxHeap.size() && maxHeap[rightChild] > maxHeap[targetChild]) {
            targetChild = rightChild;
        }
        if (targetChild != index) {
            std::swap(maxHeap[index], maxHeap[targetChild]);
            index = targetChild;
        } else {
            break;
        }
    }
  }
public:
  // Function to insert an element into the priority queue
  void enqueue(T value) {
    maxHeap.push_back(value);
    heapifyUp(maxHeap.size() - 1);
  }
  // Function to remove and return the maximum element from the priority queue
  T dequeue() {
    if (isEmpty()) {
        throw std::out_of_range("Priority Queue is empty");
    }
    T maxElement = maxHeap[0];
    maxHeap[0] = maxHeap.back();
    maxHeap.pop_back();
    heapifyDown(0);
    return maxElement;
  }
  // Function to check if the priority queue is empty
  bool isEmpty() const {
    return maxHeap.empty();
  }
};
```

```
int main() {
    // Example usage of PriorityQueue
    PriorityQueue<int> priorityQueue;
    priorityQueue.enqueue(12);
    priorityQueue.enqueue(7);
    priorityQueue.enqueue(15);
    priorityQueue.enqueue(5);
    priorityQueue.enqueue(10);
    std::cout << "Priority Queue Contents:" << std::endl;
    while (!priorityQueue.isEmpty()) {
        std::cout << priorityQueue.dequeue() << " ";
    }
    std::cout << std::endl;
    return 0;
}
```

In this example, the PriorityQueue class template provides basic priority queue operations using a max-heap. The enqueue function inserts an element into the priority queue, maintaining the max heap property using heapifyUp. The dequeue function removes and returns the maximum element from the priority queue, maintaining the max heap property using heapifyDown. The isEmpty function checks if the priority queue is empty.

The main function demonstrates the usage of the PriorityQueue class to enqueue elements and dequeue the maximum element until the priority queue is empty.

11.2. Use a priority queue to solve a real world problem like task scheduling

A real-world problem that can be solved using a priority queue is task scheduling. In task scheduling, each task has a priority, and the scheduler processes tasks based on their priorities. A priority queue can efficiently manage the order in which tasks are processed. Below is an example of using a priority queue to implement a simple task scheduler in C++:

```
#include <iostream>
#include <queue>
#include <string>
class Task {
public:
   std::string name;
   int priority;
   Task(const std::string& taskName, int taskPriority) : name(taskName),
priority(taskPriority) {}
   // Overloading the less-than operator for priority queue ordering
   bool operator<(const Task& other) const {
      // Higher priority tasks should have higher priority in the priority queue
      return priority < other.priority;
   }
};
class TaskScheduler {
private:
   std::priority_queue<Task> taskQueue;
public:
   // Function to add a task to the scheduler
   void addTask(const std::string& taskName, int taskPriority) {
      Task newTask(taskName, taskPriority);
      taskQueue.push(newTask);
      std::cout << "Task '" << taskName << "' added to the scheduler with priority " <<
taskPriority << std::endl;
   }
   // Function to process tasks in priority order
   void processTasks() {
```

```
        std::cout << "\nProcessing tasks in priority order:" << std::endl;
        while (!taskQueue.empty()) {
            Task currentTask = taskQueue.top();
            taskQueue.pop();
            std::cout << "Processing task '" << currentTask.name << "' with priority " <<
currentTask.priority << std::endl;
        }
    }
};
int main() {
    TaskScheduler scheduler;
    // Adding tasks to the scheduler
    scheduler.addTask("Task A", 3);
    scheduler.addTask("Task B", 1);
    scheduler.addTask("Task C", 2);
    scheduler.addTask("Task D", 4);
    // Processing tasks in priority order
    scheduler.processTasks();
    return 0;
}
```

In this example, the Task class represents a task with a name and a priority. The TaskScheduler class has a priority queue of tasks. The addTask method adds a new task to the scheduler, and the tasks are automatically arranged in the priority queue based on their priorities. The processTasks method dequeues tasks from the priority queue and processes them in priority order.

This example is a simplified illustration, and in a real-world scenario, tasks might have additional attributes, and the scheduling logic could be more complex. The priority queue efficiently handles the ordering of tasks based on their priorities, making it suitable for task scheduling applications.

12.DYNAMIC PROGRAMMING

12.1. Fibonacci Series

Dynamic programming can be used to efficiently compute the Fibonacci series. Below is an example of implementing the Fibonacci series using dynamic programming with a class in C++:

```
#include <iostream>
#include <vector>
class Fibonacci {
private:
    std::vector<long long> memo;
public:
    // Constructor to initialize the memoization table
    Fibonacci(int n) : memo(n + 1, -1) {}
    // Function to compute the nth Fibonacci number using memoization
    long long computeFibonacci(int n) {
        if (n <= 1) {
            return n;
        }
        // Check if the result is already memoized
        if (memo[n] != -1) {
            return memo[n];
        }
        // Compute Fibonacci number and memoize the result
        memo[n] = computeFibonacci(n - 1) + computeFibonacci(n - 2);
        return memo[n];
    }
};
int main() {
    int n;
    std::cout << "Enter the value of n for Fibonacci series: ";
    std::cin >> n;
    if (n < 0) {
        std::cout << "Please enter a non-negative value for n." << std::endl;
```

```
        return 1;
    }
    Fibonacci fib(n);
    std::cout << "Fibonacci Series up to " << n << " terms:" << std::endl;
    for (int i = 0; i <= n; ++i) {
        std::cout << fib.computeFibonacci(i) << " ";
    }
    std::cout << std::endl;
    return 0;
}
```

In this example, the Fibonacci class has a memoization table (memo) to store computed Fibonacci numbers. The computeFibonacci function uses dynamic programming and memoization to efficiently calculate the nth Fibonacci number. The results are stored in the memo table to avoid redundant computations.

The main function takes user input for the value of n (the number of terms in the Fibonacci series) and prints the Fibonacci series up to the nth term using the Fibonacci class.

The use of dynamic programming with memoization helps avoid redundant computations and improves the efficiency of calculating Fibonacci numbers. The long long data type is used to handle larger Fibonacci numbers that may exceed the range of int.

12.2. Longest common subsequence problem

The longest common subsequence (LCS) problem is a classic dynamic programming problem. Below is an example of implementing the solution using a class in C++. The class is named LongestCommonSubsequence.

```
#include <iostream>
#include <vector>
class LongestCommonSubsequence {
private:
    std::vector<std::vector<int>> memo;
public:
    // Constructor to initialize the memoization table
    LongestCommonSubsequence(int m, int n) : memo(m + 1, std::vector<int>(n + 1, -1)) {}
    // Function to calculate the length of the longest common subsequence
    int calculateLCS(const std::string& str1, const std::string& str2) {
        int m = str1.length();
        int n = str2.length();
        // Base case: if either of the strings is empty, LCS is 0
        if (m == 0 || n == 0) {
            return 0;
        }
        // Check if the result is already memoized
        if (memo[m][n] != -1) {
            return memo[m][n];
        }
        // If the last characters of both strings match
        if (str1[m - 1] == str2[n - 1]) {
            memo[m][n] = 1 + calculateLCS(str1.substr(0, m - 1), str2.substr(0, n - 1));
        } else {
            // If the last characters do not match, consider two cases:
            // 1. Exclude the last character of the first string
            // 2. Exclude the last character of the second string
            memo[m][n] = std::max(calculateLCS(str1, str2.substr(0, n - 1)),
 calculateLCS(str1.substr(0, m - 1), str2));
```

```
        }
        return memo[m][n];
    }
};
int main() {
    std::string str1, str2;
    std::cout << "Enter the first string: ";
    std::cin >> str1;
    std::cout << "Enter the second string: ";
    std::cin >> str2;
    LongestCommonSubsequence lcs(str1.length(), str2.length());
    int length = lcs.calculateLCS(str1, str2);
    std::cout << "Length of Longest Common Subsequence: " << length << std::endl;
    return 0;
}
```

In this example, the LongestCommonSubsequence class uses dynamic programming and memoization to calculate the length of the longest common subsequence. The memoization table (memo) is used to store previously computed results to avoid redundant calculations.

The calculateLCS function recursively calculates the length of the LCS based on the last characters of the two strings. The result is memoized to avoid redundant computations.

This example calculates the length of the LCS. If you also need to retrieve the actual LCS sequence, additional modifications to the code would be required.

12.3. Knapsack problem

The knapsack problem is a classic optimization problem, and it can be solved using dynamic programming. Below is an example of implementing the 0/1 knapsack problem using a class in C++. The class is named Knapsack.

```
#include <iostream>
#include <vector>
class Knapsack {
private:
  std::vector<std::vector<int>> memo;
public:
  // Constructor to initialize the memoization table
  Knapsack(int n, int capacity) : memo(n + 1, std::vector<int>(capacity + 1, -1)) {}
  // Function to solve the 0/1 knapsack problem using dynamic programming
  int knapsackDP(const std::vector<int>& weights, const std::vector<int>& values, int n, int
capacity) {
    // Base case: if either the number of items or the capacity is 0
    if (n == 0 || capacity == 0) {
      return 0;
    }
    // Check if the result is already memoized
    if (memo[n][capacity] != -1) {
      return memo[n][capacity];
    }
    // If the weight of the current item exceeds the remaining capacity,
    // skip the current item and move to the next item
    if (weights[n - 1] > capacity) {
      memo[n][capacity] = knapsackDP(weights, values, n - 1, capacity);
    } else {
      // Consider two cases:
      // 1. Include the current item
      // 2. Exclude the current item
      memo[n][capacity] = std::max(
        values[n - 1] + knapsackDP(weights, values, n - 1, capacity - weights[n - 1]),
```

```
            knapsackDP(weights, values, n - 1, capacity)
        );
    }
    return memo[n][capacity];
  }
};
int main() {
  int n, capacity;
  std::cout << "Enter the number of items: ";
  std::cin >> n;
  std::vector<int> weights(n);
  std::vector<int> values(n);
  std::cout << "Enter the weights of the items:" << std::endl;
  for (int i = 0; i < n; ++i) {
    std::cin >> weights[i];
  }
  std::cout << "Enter the values of the items:" << std::endl;
  for (int i = 0; i < n; ++i) {
    std::cin >> values[i];
  }
  std::cout << "Enter the knapsack capacity: ";
  std::cin >> capacity;
  Knapsack knapsack(n, capacity);
  int maxTotalValue = knapsack.knapsackDP(weights, values, n, capacity);
  std::cout << "Maximum total value in the knapsack: " << maxTotalValue << std::endl;
  return 0;
}
```

In this example, the Knapsack class uses dynamic programming and memoization to solve the 0/1 knapsack problem. The memoization table (memo) is used to store previously computed results to avoid redundant calculations.

The knapsackDP function recursively calculates the maximum total value that can be obtained within the given knapsack capacity. The result is memoized to avoid redundant computations.

The user is prompted to enter the number of items, the weights and values of the items, and the knapsack capacity. The program then outputs the maximum total value that can be obtained in the knapsack.

13. TRIE IMPLEMENTATION

13.1. Implement a trie data structure for efficient string storage and retrieval

A trie (pronounced "try") is a tree-like data structure used for efficient storage and retrieval of strings. Each node in the trie represents a character, and the edges represent the transitions between characters. Below is an example of implementing a trie data structure using a class in C++. The class is named Trie.

```
#include <iostream>
#include <unordered_map>
class TrieNode {
public:
  std::unordered_map<char, TrieNode*> children;
  bool isEndOfWord;
  TrieNode() : isEndOfWord(false) {}
};
class Trie {
private:
  TrieNode* root;
public:
  Trie() : root(new TrieNode()) {}
  // Function to insert a word into the trie
  void insert(const std::string& word) {
    TrieNode* current = root;
    for (char ch : word) {
      if (current->children.find(ch) == current->children.end()) {
        // Create a new node if the character is not present
        current->children[ch] = new TrieNode();
      }
      // Move to the next node
      current = current->children[ch];
    }
    // Mark the end of the word
    current->isEndOfWord = true;
  }
```

```
    // Function to search for a word in the trie
    bool search(const std::string& word) const {
        TrieNode* node = findNode(word);
        return (node != nullptr && node->isEndOfWord);
    }
    // Function to check if a word prefix exists in the trie
    bool startsWith(const std::string& prefix) const {
        return (findNode(prefix) != nullptr);
    }
private:
    // Helper function to find the last node of a word in the trie
    TrieNode* findNode(const std::string& word) const {
        TrieNode* current = root;
        for (char ch : word) {
            if (current->children.find(ch) == current->children.end()) {
                // If the character is not found, the word is not in the trie
                return nullptr;
            }
            // Move to the next node
            current = current->children[ch];
        }
        return current;
    }
};
int main() {
    // Example usage of Trie
    Trie trie;
    trie.insert("apple");
    trie.insert("app");
    trie.insert("application");
    std::cout << "Search 'app': " << (trie.search("app") ? "Found" : "Not Found") << std::endl;
    std::cout << "Search 'appl': " << (trie.search("appl") ? "Found" : "Not Found") <<
std::endl;
```

```
    std::cout << "StartsWith 'app': " << (trie.startsWith("app") ? "Found" : "Not Found") <<
std::endl;
    return 0;
}
```

In this example, the TrieNode class represents a node in the trie, and the Trie class provides methods for inserting, searching, and checking prefixes. The trie is implemented using a hash map to efficiently represent the children of each node.

The insert function inserts a word into the trie, creating nodes as needed. The search function checks if a word exists in the trie, and the startsWith function checks if a word prefix exists.

The example demonstrates creating a trie, inserting words, and performing searches and prefix checks. Adjustments can be made to add more functionality or optimize the implementation further.

13.2.Use a trie implement an auto complete feature

Implementing an autocomplete feature using a trie is a practical use case. Below is an example of implementing an autocomplete feature using a trie data structure in C++. The class is named AutocompleteTrie.

```
#include <iostream>
#include <unordered_map>
#include <vector>
class TrieNode {
public:
   std::unordered_map<char, TrieNode*> children;
   bool isEndOfWord;
   TrieNode() : isEndOfWord(false) {}
};
class AutocompleteTrie {
private:
   TrieNode* root;
public:
   AutocompleteTrie() : root(new TrieNode()) {}
   // Function to insert a word into the autocomplete trie
   void insert(const std::string& word) {
      TrieNode* current = root;
      for (char ch : word) {
         if (current->children.find(ch) == current->children.end()) {
            // Create a new node if the character is not present
            current->children[ch] = new TrieNode();
         }
         // Move to the next node
         current = current->children[ch];
      }
      // Mark the end of the word
      current->isEndOfWord = true;
   }
   // Function to find all words with a given prefix
```

```
    std::vector<std::string> autocomplete(const std::string& prefix) const {
        TrieNode* prefixNode = findNode(prefix);
        std::vector<std::string> suggestions;
        if (prefixNode != nullptr) {
            // Perform a depth-first traversal to find all words with the given prefix
            autocompleteHelper(prefixNode, prefix, suggestions);
        }
        return suggestions;
    }
private:
    // Helper function for autocomplete to perform depth-first traversal
    void autocompleteHelper(TrieNode* node, const std::string& currentPrefix,
std::vector<std::string>& suggestions) const {
        if (node->isEndOfWord) {
            // If the current node represents the end of a word, add it to suggestions
            suggestions.push_back(currentPrefix);
        }
        for (const auto& child : node->children) {
            // Recursively traverse each child node
            autocompleteHelper(child.second, currentPrefix + child.first, suggestions);
        }
    }
    // Helper function to find the last node of a prefix in the trie
    TrieNode* findNode(const std::string& prefix) const {
        TrieNode* current = root;
        for (char ch : prefix) {
            if (current->children.find(ch) == current->children.end()) {
                // If the character is not found, the prefix is not in the trie
                return nullptr;
            }
            // Move to the next node
            current = current->children[ch];
        }
```

```
        return current;
    }
};
int main() {
    // Example usage of AutocompleteTrie
    AutocompleteTrie autocompleteTrie;
    // Insert words into the autocomplete trie
    autocompleteTrie.insert("apple");
    autocompleteTrie.insert("app");
    autocompleteTrie.insert("application");
    autocompleteTrie.insert("banana");
    // Perform autocomplete for a given prefix
    std::string prefix;
    std::cout << "Enter a prefix for autocomplete: ";
    std::cin >> prefix;
    std::vector<std::string> suggestions = autocompleteTrie.autocomplete(prefix);
    // Display autocomplete suggestions
    if (!suggestions.empty()) {
        std::cout << "Autocomplete suggestions for '" << prefix << "':" << std::endl;
        for (const auto& suggestion : suggestions) {
            std::cout << suggestion << std::endl;
        }
    } else {
        std::cout << "No autocomplete suggestions found for '" << prefix << "'" << std::endl;
    }
    return 0;
}
```

In this example, the AutocompleteTrie class extends the basic trie functionality to provide autocomplete suggestions for a given prefix. The autocomplete function finds all words with the given prefix by performing a depth-first traversal.

The main function demonstrates creating an AutocompleteTrie, inserting words, and performing autocomplete for a user-entered prefix. The program then displays the autocomplete suggestions.

You can extend this example further to include additional features or integrate it into a larger application.

14. ADVANCED TOPICS

14.1. Disjoint set data structure

The disjoint-set data structure, also known as the union-find data structure, is often used to efficiently manage a partition of a set into disjoint subsets. It supports two main operations: finding which subset a particular element belongs to and merging two subsets. Here's an example of implementing a disjoint-set data structure using a class in C++:

```
#include <iostream>
#include <unordered_map>
#include <vector>
class DisjointSet {
private:
   std::unordered_map<int, int> parent;
   std::unordered_map<int, int> rank;
public:
   // Function to make a set with a single element
   void makeSet(int element) {
      parent[element] = element;
      rank[element] = 0;
   }
   // Function to find the representative (root) of the set to which an element belongs
   int findSet(int element) {
      // Path compression
      if (parent[element] != element) {
         parent[element] = findSet(parent[element]);
      }
      return parent[element];
   }
   // Function to merge two sets
   void unionSets(int element1, int element2) {
      int root1 = findSet(element1);
      int root2 = findSet(element2);
      // Union by rank
      if (root1 != root2) {
```

```
            if (rank[root1] < rank[root2]) {
                parent[root1] = root2;
            } else if (rank[root1] > rank[root2]) {
                parent[root2] = root1;
            } else {
                parent[root1] = root2;
                rank[root2]++;
            }
        }
    }
};
int main() {
    DisjointSet disjointSet;
    // Create sets with single elements
    for (int i = 1; i <= 5; ++i) {
        disjointSet.makeSet(i);
    }
    // Perform union operations
    disjointSet.unionSets(1, 2);
    disjointSet.unionSets(2, 3);
    disjointSet.unionSets(4, 5);
    // Test if elements belong to the same set
    std::cout << "1 and 3 belong to the same set: " << (disjointSet.findSet(1) ==
disjointSet.findSet(3) ? "Yes" : "No") << std::endl;
    std::cout << "1 and 5 belong to the same set: " << (disjointSet.findSet(1) ==
disjointSet.findSet(5) ? "Yes" : "No") << std::endl;
    return 0; }
```

In this example, the DisjointSet class provides the makeSet, findSet, and unionSets operations. The makeSet function initializes a set with a single element, findSet finds the representative (root) of the set to which an element belongs with path compression, and unionSets merges two sets based on their ranks.

The main function demonstrates creating sets, performing union operations, and testing whether elements belong to the same set. Adjustments can be made to incorporate additional features or integrate the disjoint-set data structure into a larger application.

14.2. LRU cache

An LRU (Least Recently Used) cache is a data structure that maintains a fixed-size set of items. When the cache reaches its capacity, the least recently used item is evicted to make room for new items. Here's an example of implementing an LRU cache using a class in C++:

```
#include <iostream>
#include <unordered_map>
#include <list>
class LRUCache {
private:
    int capacity;
    std::unordered_map<int, std::pair<int, std::list<int>::iterator>> cacheMap;
    std::list<int> recentlyUsed;
public:
    LRUCache(int cap) : capacity(cap) {}
    // Function to get the value of the key from the cache
    int get(int key) {
        if (cacheMap.find(key) == cacheMap.end()) {
            // Key not present in the cache
            return -1;
        }
        // Move the accessed key to the front of the recentlyUsed list
        recentlyUsed.erase(cacheMap[key].second);
        recentlyUsed.push_front(key);
        cacheMap[key].second = recentlyUsed.begin();
        return cacheMap[key].first;
    }
    // Function to insert a key-value pair into the cache
    void put(int key, int value) {
        if (cacheMap.find(key) != cacheMap.end()) {
            // Key already present, update the value and move to the front of recentlyUsed list
            recentlyUsed.erase(cacheMap[key].second);
            recentlyUsed.push_front(key);
            cacheMap[key] = {value, recentlyUsed.begin()};
```

```
        } else {
            // Cache is at capacity, evict the least recently used item
            if (cacheMap.size() == capacity) {
                int lruKey = recentlyUsed.back();
                recentlyUsed.pop_back();
                cacheMap.erase(lruKey);
            }
            // Insert the new key-value pair
            recentlyUsed.push_front(key);
            cacheMap[key] = {value, recentlyUsed.begin()};
        }
    }
};
int main() {
    // Example usage of LRUCache
    LRUCache lruCache(2);
    lruCache.put(1, 1);
    lruCache.put(2, 2);
    std::cout << "Value for key 1: " << lruCache.get(1) << std::endl; // Output: 1
    lruCache.put(3, 3);
    std::cout << "Value for key 2: " << lruCache.get(2) << std::endl; // Output: -1 (not found)
    std::cout << "Value for key 3: " << lruCache.get(3) << std::endl; // Output: 3
    return 0;
}
```

In this example, the LRUCache class uses a combination of an unordered map (cacheMap) and a doubly-linked list (recentlyUsed) to efficiently implement the LRU cache. The unordered map is used to store key-value pairs along with their positions in the linked list. The linked list is used to maintain the order of recently used keys.

The get function retrieves the value for a given key from the cache, updating the order in the linked list to reflect the recent usage. The put function inserts a new key-value pair or updates an existing one, evicting the least recently used item if the cache is at capacity.

The main function demonstrates example usage of the LRUCache. Adjustments can be made to change the cache capacity or incorporate additional features based on specific requirements.

www.ingramcontent.com/pod-product-compliance
Lightning Source LLC
Chambersburg PA
CBHW040743170726
48282CB00023B/124
9789361287244